International Students' Experience in UK Higher Education

(A HANDBOOK FOR INTERNATIONAL STUDENTS AND THOSE WORKING WITH THEM)

Eunice Okorocha, PhD

About the Author

Dr Eunice Okorocha did her PhD at the Department of Educational Studies of The University of Surrey, England. She is the author of _Supervising International Research Students_ published by Society for Research into Higher Education.(SRHE) 1st Edition 1997 and 2nd Edition 2007. _Crossing Cultures_ (2004) published by Transfiguration Press. Also _Cultural Issues in Working with International Students_ (April 2010) and _Counselling International Students_ (April 2010) published by Arima Publishing UK.

The author is a Cultural Awareness Trainer who had run Cultural Awareness Workshops in Several Universities and Institution of Higher Learning in the UK. She has several journal articles (see Bibliography) and had presented papers at SRHE and UKCOSA (now The Council for International Education) annual conferences as well as at the European Conference of Association for Student Counselling.

She hopes this research based book will benefit international students and all who work with them. She would very much appreciate constructive comments and suggestions on how it could be improved in future editions. She can be contacted through email with this address: eiokorocha@yahoo.co.uk

Acknowledgments

I want to thank God for His grace and strength that enabled me to carry out such an extensive research from which these books have been published.

I appreciate the support of my family and friends.

I also appreciate the letter from the British Library which has given me a great motivation to publish the Research Thesis so that many will have access to the findings and recommendations. The letter sent to Surrey University by the British Library says: 'The thesis has been identified by the British library as being of high scholarly value.'

I acknowledge the publishers of my first book- The Society for Research into higher Education (SRHE) who went on to publish a second edition because of the demand for it. They acknowledged that, 'We found the first edition of Eunice's Guide 'Supervising International Research Students' quite unique The Guide presents issues which have remained fairly constant through the decades of the existence of research degree programmes.'

I agree that the issues presented in the Thesis and in these books drawn from the research have remained fairly constant over the years. For instance, issues of communication and learning across cultures will always be relevant and of great interest to all those who work with international students in institution of higher learning as Academic and Support services Staff, as well as to the students themselves.

I would like to point out that the few outstanding changes, I have noticed, are the introduction of the internet and mobile phones which have made it possible for international students to contact home and family easily, which is a positive thing. Food items from different parts of the world are much more available now in the UK than before, which is also good.

However, International Students' fees have more than trebled which may discourage some parents and students on three levels - global economic crunch, the fact that there are many more Universities in overseas countries than before leading to more choices. Moreover, many European countries have opened their shores and doors to international students by offering language schools and courses in English. This has lead to more competition for the recruitment of international students. So institutions will do well to see that they offer their international students value for money.

International Students' Experience in UK Higher Education

A research based investigation of the Academic, Personal, Social and Cultural Experience of Undergraduate and Postgraduate International Students, with recommendation for Coping Strategies

Eunice Okorocha, PhD.

2010

Published 2010 by arima publishing

www.arimapublishing.com

ISBN 978 1 84549 443 8

© Eunice Okorocha 2010

All rights reserved

This book is copyright. Subject to statutory exception and to provisions of relevant collective licensing agreements, no part of this publication may be reproduced, stored in a retrieval system, or transmitted in any form or by any means, without the prior written permission of the author.

Printed and bound in the United Kingdom

Typeset in Garamond 12/14

This book is sold subject to the conditions that it shall not, by way of trade or otherwise, be lent, re-sold, hired out, or otherwise circulated without the publisher's prior consent in any form of binding or cover other than that which it is published and without a similar condition including this condition being imposed on the subsequent purchaser.

Abramis is an imprint of arima publishing.

arima publishing
ASK House, Northgate Avenue
Bury St Edmunds, Suffolk IP32 6BB
t: (+44) 01284 700321

www.arimapublishing.com

Contents

Preface	11
Introduction	13
The International Students' Experience	17
Chapter One Extensive literature Review on International or Overseas Students' Experience	19
Chapter Two Adaptation and Adjustment Issues	29
Chapter Three Presentation of Findings on International/Overseas Students' Experience	37
Chapter Four Discussions of the Findings on International Students' Experience	57
Chapter Five Counselling Service	67
Chapter Six Barriers to Counselling International Students	73
Chapter Seven Findings on Counselling Services	81
Chapter Eight International Postgraduate Students' Experience	91
Chapter Nine Group Interview with Theological Students	99
Chapter Ten Group Interviews of Turkish Muslim Students	103

Chapter Eleven
Individual Interviews of three overseas members of staff who
'recently' completed their PhD and were employed in Universities
in the UK   107

Chapter Twelve
Conclusion and Recommendations   121

Bibliography from the Research   135

Preface

This book is based on the author's PhD study on the experience of international/overseas students and issues that affect counselling and working with them. The research was a challenging investigation which brought me into contact with a host of overseas students, counsellors and institution staff across the UK. Much more contact than can be recorded but these have enriched my personal experience and have been an adventure in human relations. The fact that all the experiences cannot be statistically tabulated reminds me of Einstein's alleged motto that:

'Not everything that counts can be counted and not everything that can be counted counts'

In looking at the experience of students from other cultures and counsellors and staff working cross-culturally, it is crucial to see the importance of individual experiences and group experiences. The level of misinterpretation and misunderstanding between people from diverse academic, cultural, religious and communication backgrounds cannot be over emphasised. This is because even within the same background words and actions can be misread depending on a number of factors which include context and attitudes of those engaged in the encounter.

As an international person who has studied, worked and ministered in different cultures I agree with Augsbuger (1986) that:

'To be cultural effective is a gift, a gift received through learning from other cultures, through being teachable in encounters with those who differ, and through coming to esteem other world-views equally with one's own.'

Overseas Students will therefore need to learn to adjust to the new system (without losing their identity) and staff who work with them will need to be aware and sensitive to a range of academic, cultural, religious and communication backgrounds.

Dr Eunice Okorocha
Email:eiokorocha@yahoo.co.uk

INTRODUCTION

The objective of the thesis (from which this book is produced) was to investigate the academic, personal and social experiences of students from overseas as they study in the United Kingdom (UK). This includes an investigation of the sources which extend assistance to them and the extent to which they avail themselves of counselling about problems of adjustment to life and study in the UK. A further purpose was to explore the issues that affect working with them especially those issues which create barriers for counsellors and staff (academic and non-academic) as they work with international/overseas students.

The <u>investigation</u> was carried out in ten universities and two theological institutions in the UK. The research is presented in three distinct, yet connected, parts: problems of adjustment, counselling services and other forms of help and co-operation. Each part comprises a literature review, presentation and discussion of findings as well as recommendations for improvement in the help given.

<u>Three perspectives</u> are explored, viz. Overseas students' views, counsellors' views and the views of staff (both academic and non-academic), by a combination of qualitative and quantitative approaches and these perspectives are related through the extensive use of triangulation.

<u>Similarities</u> were found in the perspectives as reported by the three groups of respondents in regard both to the problems of overseas students and the barriers in the operation of counselling and other services. These problems and barriers were seen to arise from differences in academic systems and expectations, from differences in cultures, and from difficulties of language and understanding.

The findings show that all three groups of respondents consider that the experiences of international/overseas students can and should be made more satisfactory by

- increased awareness of overseas students' problems of adjustment.
- the issues which create barriers in working with them.
- Provision of structured assistance to help overseas students to adjust to the British system of education and social life without losing their cultural identities.
- Assistance to counsellors and staff in acquiring or improving their cross-cultural skills to work more effectively with overseas students.
- Employment of at least one overseas person with whom students can identify in each support services team.
- Demonstration that institutions offer value for money in the educational services they provide together with sound support services enabling students to make effective use of the facilities provided. (If claims made during the marketing process are seen by the students to be justified in the outcome, the goodwill established will be beneficial not only to the institution concerned but also to the host country.)

Recommendations based on these findings are made to:

-Staff, counsellors and the institutions in which they function in order

a) To improve the experiences of overseas students.

b) To enhance the effectiveness of the services they provide

-Students' unions in order

a) To raise awareness of overseas students' experiences

b) To facilitate the integration of overseas students with home (UK) students.

-Current and future overseas students in order

a) To enable them to develop strategies to cope with life and study in the UK.

This book on the Experience of International Students will be followed by two books on: The Experience of Academic and Non-Academic Staff as well as Counsellors' views.

THE INTERNATIONAL STUDENTS' EXPERIENCE

Research Outline
This research study investigated the Academic, Personal, Social and cultural experiences of International Students and these are presented as a review of related literature on International Students' Experience, the research findings, and the discussion of the implications of the findings.

The **Research Questions** for the study were:
1. What problems (academic, personal, social and cultural) do International students experience?
2. To whom do International students turn for assistance?
3. What is the level of International students' uptake of counselling for their problems?
4. What do International students see as issues that create barriers to the help they receive?

These questions were investigated through individual interviews, surveys and group interviews. The study was predominantly a qualitative investigation with the quantitative method used as a means of knowing how wide-spread the findings are. The methods used for analysing the findings are (a) the qualitative and ethnographic summary for the interview data and (b) frequency tables as statistical analysis for the questionnaire data. The sampling strategy is purposive sampling which seeks out 'information-rich' cases.

The terms International, Overseas, Foreign, and Students from abroad are used interchangeably throughout this book.

CHAPTER ONE
EXTENSIVE LITERATURE REVIEW ON INTERNATIONAL OR OVERSEAS STUDENTS' EXPERIENCE

1.1 Historical background

The historical background of the changes that have affected the reception, movements and welfare needs of students from abroad helps in the assessment of the experience of overseas students over the years.

The history of the presence of overseas students in institutions of higher education appears to date as far back as the 13th century, according to a statement attributed to Henry the 111 in 1231 urging the inhabitants of Cambridge to treat them as welcome quests:

Unless you conduct yourselves with more restraint and moderation towards them [overseas students], they will be driven into abandoning their studies and leaving the country, which we by no means desire (Kinnell 1990:1).

Concerns for overseas students in Britain in more recent times date from Lee-Warner Committee Report of 1907. The committee looked into the need to provide information on educational matters in the home country and to advise on educational and financial as well as welfare matters once the student has reached the host country. In the 1920s, 1930s and 1940s the welfare support offered by voluntary organisations steadily developed. In the 1950s it was asserted that students from abroad arrived in the UK with high expectations:

Students from developing countries, where comparable higher education was unavailable, arrived with high expectations of British education and the British way of life (Political and Economic Planning, 20 1954:374).

Studies in the 1960s focused on the social realities the overseas students faced, which were listed as prejudice of one kind or another, welfare needs, culture shock, language difficulties and different approach to learning and teaching (Kinnell 1990). The growing needs of overseas students studying in the United Kingdom were recognised in 1968 when the United Kingdom Council for Overseas Student Affairs (UKCOSA) was established. According to Hughes and Read (1991), there was a steady flow of overseas students into the UK and in 1970/1971 the number was 32,000. At its peak in 1979/80 the number had risen to 88,000. There has been a steady increase since then.

The status of overseas students in the UK has been affected by some factors which include governmental policy on full-cost fees, market forces and changes in higher education. The issues raised in this study are highlighted in this statement by Howarth (1991:9) which emphasises the experience of most people who study away from home:

No one would say that the life of any student in this country, home or overseas, is entirely trouble free. All students will to some extent find that they will need to acclimatise and adjust to different demands and obligations but the overseas student will have special needs which the responsible institution will make an effort to anticipate and meet.

1. 2. International/Overseas Students' Problems

Pedersen (1991) argued that overseas students are likely to experience more problems than students in general and have access to fewer resources to help them. According to Dillard (1983), although overseas student exchange programmes in the USA attempt to provide a positive environment, the actual cultural context on campuses frequently generates stress, depression, frustration, fear and pessimism. As a result, he says, the adaptation process of overseas students has become one of the major concerns of some researchers in the US.

The magnitude of the difficulties a student studying in a different country and culture can encounter is described by Pedersen (1991:12):

A person's self-esteem and self-image are validated by significant others, who provide emotional and social support in culturally patterned ways. Moving to a foreign culture suddenly deprives a person of these support systems. A normal response to the withdrawing of support is anxiety, ranging from irritation and mild annoyance to the panic of extreme pain and feelings of disorientation which accompany being lost. Every decision now requires a deliberate effort and concentrated energy.

He also emphasised that these rules have been learned over a lifetime by locals. Overseas students provide an example of a population that must learn a wide range of culturally defined and typically unfamiliar roles in a short time under conditions of considerable stress.

An earlier study on students' problems (Okorocha 1990), shows that students who study in their home country also experience some problems. The argument here is that overseas students, while sharing the difficulties and problems of home students, have additional ones because they are studying very far from home and in a different culture. Other studies confirm that overseas students have more difficulty than home students in dealing with the new academic and social environment. (Cox, 1988; Furnharm and Bochner, 1982).

Some of the difficulties of overseas students which are frequently mentioned in literature will now be discussed in more detail.

Among the problems experienced by overseas students suggested by Schild (1962); Perkins et al. (1977); Animashawun (1963); Anumonye (1970); Bochner (1972); NACOSA (1988); Klineberg and Hull, (1979); Sen, (1970); Harris (1997); and Furnham (1997) are culture shock, language difficulties, financial problems, physical and health issues, emotional and family concerns.

According to Furnham and Tresize (1983) problems facing overseas students are threefold: (a) problem of living in a foreign culture which include racial discrimination, language problems, accommodation difficulties, separation reactions, dietary restrictions, financial stress and loneliness; (b) problem of late-adolescents/young adults asserting their emotional and intellectual independence; (c) and the academic problems associated with higher educational study.

Some of these problems mentioned in literature on overseas students' experience are discussed in greater details below:

1.3. Culture shock

Culture shock rates high as a major item in literature on overseas students' problems. The term was first attributed to Oberg (1958) who suggested that this condition is precipitated by the anxiety that results from losing one's familiar signs and symbols of social interaction, that is, losing the sense of when and how to do the right things. Bock (1970) describes culture shock as an emotional reaction caused by an inability to understand, control or predict another person's behaviour. Alder (1975) explains culture shock as a set of emotional reactions to the loss of one's culture which often leads to a constant feeling of helplessness, confusion and panic. Simply put, culture shock is that odd feeling people have in a new environment when all familiar supports seem to have been knocked from under them. Culture shock can thus place great stress on a person's personality and stability and can present a threat to his/her identity. As a result of a major review of the literature on the psychological adjustment of sojourners, Church (1982)concludes that culture shock is a normal process of adaptation to cultural stress, which involves symptoms such as anxiety, irritability and a longing for a more predictable environment.

Thus a person in an unfamiliar social environment is confused and apparently apathetic until he or she has had time to develop a new set of cognitive constructs to understand and enact the appropriate behaviour (Furnham 1997). Adler (1975) suggests that although culture shock is often associated with negative consequences, it may, in mild doses, be useful for self-development and personal growth. Thus culture shock may be seen as a transitional experience which can result in the adoption of new values, attitudes and behaviour patterns.

According to Furnham (1997) the quality and quantity of culture shock has been shown to be related to the extent of difference between the sojourners' culture and the culture of country they are visiting. Some studies suggest that, as sojourners, overseas students are likely to experience culture shock. (Klineberg and Hull, 1979; Church, 1982). Furnham and Bochner (1986) recommend that the negative aspects of culture shock can be ameliorated through programmes of cultural orientation.

1.4. Homesickness

Furnham (1997:17) describes the key psychological features of homesickness as a strong preoccupation with the thought of home, a perceived need to go home, a sense of grief for the people, place and things at home; and a concurrent feeling of unhappiness, dis-ease and disorientation in the new place which is conspicuously not home.

Fisher et al. (1985) identified a link between homesickness reporting and a greater number of cognitive failures, poor concentration, handing in work late and decrements in work quality. They suggested that homesickness may exercise a considerable influence on academic performance, at least over a short time.

1.5. Language difficulties

Klineberg and Hull (1979) conducted a study of overseas students at foreign universities in eleven countries and identified language difficulties as one of the major problems experienced by students studying overseas. For most, English is a foreign, and second or third language. It has been observed by the British Council (1991) that a foreigner who speaks English - however badly - deserves respect because he/she speaks at least one other language. Many overseas students are studying in their third or fourth language.

According to Elton (1985), language problems experienced by overseas students vary considerably and it is necessary to distinguish between those students for whom English is a 'foreign' language and those for whom it is a 'second' language. Foreign language users, e.g. students from Middle East, Latin America and Europe, learned English as an academic subject, while Second language users like most students from the Commonwealth countries have used English as a medium of education. Elton (1985) further observes that reading presents the least difficulties but adequate and suitable styles are often problems in students' written English. He points out that those who have not studied in English before are at a particular disadvantage.

Cortazzi and Jin (1997:79) suggest that students who come from different cultural backgrounds will often use different styles of communication in English, even when they have attained very high language competence.

They further argue that Cultural ways of speaking and writing are transferred from other languages to English, especially those ways which are taken for granted. For instance:

Whereas grammar and vocabulary are obvious areas which may need attention, other aspects of cultures of communication may be overlooked, for example uses of intonation, pauses, eye contact, body language, rhetorical patterns and ways of presenting information.

They also note the other challenges of differences in communication such as those that lead to wrong assessments of those who use them; for example, Middle East students often use heavy intonation, relatively loud voices and rhetorical exaggeration which are acceptable and often desirable in their native Arabic but they may be seen by British tutors and students (quite wrongly) as overbearing or aggressive.

Other customary responses cited by Cortazzi and Jin (1997) include 'pauses in turn-taking', how 'yes' and 'no' can function differently in different languages, 'deductive' and 'inductive' discourse patterns. The later is whether a main idea is introduced first, followed by background information and supporting arguments, or vice versa. They argue that, whereas British tutors will probably prefer the former, Chinese students (and some other overseas students) will more naturally use the later.

1.6. Academic Problems

Elton (1985) suggests that learning styles relate to problems of earlier experience and expectations. The experience of academic work in their own country may lead some overseas students to adopt study methods different from, and sometimes inappropriate, to study in the host country. Students who had their earlier education in a different system might have their own styles and conventions on learning: for example, deference to teaching staff which could inhibit the debate and discussion that was often coupled with an expectation that lengthy passages of text should be committed to memory and reproduced at appropriate time which could be interpreted as 'plagiarism' (1985:12).

According to Cortazzi and Jin (1997) a culture of learning depends on the norms, values and expectations of teachers and learners relative to classroom activity; as an example they cited their investigation of Chinese culture of learning. They found that the students expected the tutor to have deep knowledge as an authority and an expert. This knowledge is transmitted to students who are expected to internalise it. They expect the tutor to be caring and helpful while they reciprocate by respecting the teacher. They suggest that Chinese students may be disappointed or disillusioned if they observe British teachers who do not seem, in their eyes, to carry out their part of the reciprocal relationship.

They further argue that, where western teachers sometimes see Chinese students as 'passive', they should realise that the Chinese culture of learning includes the need to listen and reflect and probably not to volunteer comments unless asked. Learning, they say, involves intensive memorisation - which is often brushed aside as rote-learning by western tutors - but which Chinese regard as a stage in learning that will lead to understanding later after a period of hard work.

1.7. Psycho-social problems

Zwingmann et al. (1983) have identified isolation, loneliness and stress as problems of 'uprooting' that may affect the health and, subsequently, the academic performance of students from abroad. They reported case studies of individuals with severe psychological disturbance triggered by uprooting.

Furnham (1997) argues that there is enough consistent literature to indicate that there is a relationship between social support and psychological disorder, suggesting that the various types of support provided by interpersonal relationships play a crucial role in determining a person's general adaptive functioning and sense of well-being.

For the overseas students, moving to a different country involves leaving behind family, friends and acquaintances such as work colleagues and neighbours. As a result supportive relationships with family and friends are no longer available to the same extent to sustain them. If this is not recognised and provided for, it may lead to increase in physical and mental stress (Furnham 1997).

1.8. Other Problems

Two other problems frequently mentioned include finding familiar food items and finding suitable accommodation (Kinnell 1990). Church (1982) suggests that the problems that students report when studying abroad remain consistent but differ in degree between different cultures. Anumonye (1970) and Singh (1963) have drawn attention to the negative effects of prejudice and discrimination on students' psychological health. Elton (1985) suggested that common experience of prejudice and condescension exacerbated overseas students' feeling of alienation.

CHAPTER TWO
ADAPTATION AND ADJUSTMENT ISSUES

2.1. After the extensive discussion of some predominant problems of overseas students what now follows is a review of some literature on their adaptation and adjustment processes.

According to Dillard (1983) the adaptation process of overseas students has become an important issue to those who assist them. Pedersen (1991) states that firstly, when overseas students arrive at overseas universities, the circumstances suddenly and simultaneously impose a variety of competing and sometimes contradictory roles, and secondly, when the requirements of those roles are realistically perceived and effectively learned, the student's experience is likely to be 'successful'. However, when the roles are not accommodated, the resulting identity diffusion and role conflict may also affect the student's emotional well-being, and present serious obstacles to the achievement of educational objectives. Citing Spradley and Philips (1972), Pedersen (1991:10) concludes:

Although international students come from widely diverse backgrounds, they are expected to adjust to a narrowly defined set of behaviours requiring them to learn their new and 'proper' roles very rapidly. Failure to learn their new roles will result in confusion about their own identity and create conflict. Role-learning then becomes a necessary coping strategy.

According to him the lack of adequate theory on the adjustment of overseas students has been a major factor inhibiting research. He cited David (1972), Church (1982) and Kelley (1988) who argued that an over-emphasis on identifying adjustment problems or successful outcomes, without exploring the dynamics or process of adjustment itself, has inhibited the development of theories. According to Pedersen the overseas student is confronted with two important questions: (1) Is my cultural identity of any value and is it to be retained? (2) Are positive relations with the larger dominant society to be sought? He further said that answers to these questions will determine whether :

The international student experiences assimilation, integration, rejection or deculturation. Assimilation means relinquishing cultural identity and moving into the larger society. Integration implies maintenance of cultural integrity while also becoming a part of the larger social framework. Rejection refers to withdrawal from the larger society or being segregated from the larger society. Deculturation refers to feeling of alienation, loss of identity and high levels of a culturative stress; the student has lost contact with both the home and host culture (Pedersen1991:16).

The three phases of acculturation are typically described as contact, conflict and adaptation (first linked with Lysgaard 1955). This U-shape model describes acculturation over time: first the initial excitement and optimism in the course of contact, second the feeling of failure and depression, and third the recovery to a new level of excitement and optimism.

The model was later modified by Gullahorn et al. (1966) in an application of this principle described as W-curve to accommodate both the acculturation to the host culture and the re-acculturation after the student returns home. Eleven studies reviewed by Church (1982) support the U-curve hypothesis but suggest that accommodation does not lead to a recovery at the original level of positive functioning. Five other studies that failed to support the U-curve were also reviewed by Church. They show the absence of cross-sectional support for the basic thesis. His conclusion is that support for the U-curve hypothesis is weak and over-generalised.

Furnham and Bochner (1986) identified some problems with the U-curve hypothesis. They suggested that there were many dependent variables to consider as aspects of adjustment, such as depression, loneliness, homesickness and other attitudes. Their view is that a more fruitful approach for future research might be to focus on interpersonal rather than intrapersonal variables.

A study of the adjustment issues of overseas students in the UK was conducted at Loughborough University by Mackinlay and Stevenson (1994). Their findings indicate that the typical adjustment pattern of overseas students did not conform to the U-curve. They said that from the information in their study the overseas students' experience is much more complex and is related more to the personal and social factors affecting each individual. Nearly all subjects in their study reported that the most difficult time was the first few days. Rather than experiencing an initial 'honeymoon' period many students were totally disoriented at the start of their time in the UK.

Parr, Bradley & Bingi (1992) conducted a study in the USA on the concerns and feelings of overseas students which showed that, although these students seem to be a resilient group, homesickness and loneliness are pervasive and depression common. They noted that students with better language competence experience less discomfort than do students with poor language competence. According to their findings, differences in the background and characteristics of overseas students seem to influence their adjustment. Acculturative stress increases as the gap between the student's traditional culture and the host culture grows. Students from western countries adjust more easily than students from the non-western countries. This is not surprising because students from European countries often are used to climate and diet more similar to the UK condition.

In the review of older studies, Parr et al. (1992) noted that flexibility, non-authoritarianism, empathy, and high self-esteem correlated positively with positive adjustment. One of the greatest concerns of overseas students, according to them, was how to adapt to cultural differences, without sacrificing their own cultural norms. They concluded that overseas students have the ability to persevere, sometimes despite what may seem like insurmountable odds. Furnham and Bochner (1986) recommended that the major task of the student is not to adjust to the new culture but to learn its salient characteristics. Adjustment will, therefore, involve training the overseas students in appropriate skills.

In a study on the adjustment problems of overseas student groups, Perkins et al. (1977) refer to adjustment problems as problems of academic and personal or social nature experienced by overseas students in the USA. In this study carried out in the University of Georgia, they found that Chinese students most frequently noted the use of English language as a problem, while the students from India noted finances and dating, etc.. Their conclusion was that, although overseas students have some problems in common, they also have problems peculiar to their own national groups.

2.2 Gender issue in Adjustment

According to Manese et al. (1988), Goldsmith, (1985) published studies on sex differences among overseas students are very limited and show mixed results. They cited a study by Porter which found that women reported having more problems than men. This was contrasted with another study by Collins (in Lee et al. 1981) which found the opposite. The Manese et al. study indicated that there were differences in perceptions and needs of male and female overseas undergraduate students, with females expecting harder times at the institution and being more easily discouraged than males.

2.3. Cultural Orientation and Staff Awareness Workshops as some methods of understanding and assisting international students in the adaptation process.

A few studies have looked at what can be done to assist overseas students in their adaptation process. Some of the suggestions include cultural orientation and raising staff awareness as discussed below.

A study on adaptation of overseas students carried out in Canada by Heikinheimo and Shutte (1986) reported that adaptation is a process that blends academic, social, financial, cultural and linguistic elements. Using qualitative methodology, the authors found that overseas students found language skills, academic issues and social interaction to be the most difficult adjustment problems. They recommended that overseas students should be encouraged to adopt a receptive and open view concerning their life-style in the host country. They also said that, because many adaptation problems of overseas students remain relatively unknown to academic and support staff of university and colleges, workshops should be arranged for university personnel who are in contact with overseas students to help them to understand their adaptation problems and to develop encouraging and supportive response patterns.

One way a few institutions of higher education have responded to adaptation and adjustment problems experienced by overseas students is to provide initial cultural orientation (McKinlay 1993). An exploratory study, conducted at the Loughborough University in 1993 by McKinlay, Pattison & Gross, investigated the psychological effects of a cultural orientation course on postgraduate overseas students. The hypothesis was that a group that attended a pre-sessional course would experience less culture shock than a group that did not. Three quantitative measures were used - Langner 22-item Questionnaire (a measure of mental health), the Dundee Relocation Inventory, and an Overseas Student Questionnaire devised for that particular study.

McKinlay et al. found that overseas students in the pre-sessional group were significantly more homesick than overseas students in the standard arrival group. Its members were said to have reported a higher level of psychological distress and a more negative evaluation of their experiences in the UK. The hypothesis was therefore rejected. They concluded that the experience of overseas students is much more complex and is more related to personal and social factors affecting each individual. They recommended the development of coherent management strategies to support overseas students and to address their needs all year round.

2.4. Student-Centred Induction

Jenkins (1990) described a student-centred which was a contrast, in his experience, to the old format of institution-centred induction. He said the problem with the old format, of a lecture room and a lecture-style approach, was that it tended to rely on a one-way communication system on his terms, his space and his agenda. It was also a one-off approach and if some students could not be there for any reason, there were no arrangements for catching up later.

The student-centred approach which he later adopted used a spacious teaching room in the library which was booked for a whole week and he moved his office there for the period. This location was department-neutral (not attached to any department) and the library was easy for overseas student to find. He said this was ideal because it allowed a two-way communication on the students' terms, with the students' agenda, in the students' time and in the students' space. The students were able to ask questions individually as well as come and go as often as they wanted. The reception centre became a drop-in centre.

Jenkins (1990) concluded that this change in induction format made it possible to assist more students and help them to work out what they wanted to do with the information available. The student-centred approach made the students more productive and alive, in contrast with the old approach which expected them to be receptive and passive. The student-oriented induction attracted hundreds of new students at different times to whom more personal attention was given while the old approach had attracted only about a dozen new arrivals.

Summary

This review of literature on international/overseas students has looked at problems. It has also looked at some adaptation and adjustment issues.

CHAPTER THREE
PRESENTATION OF FINDINGS ON INTERNATIONAL/OVERSEAS STUDENTS' EXPERIENCE

3. 1 Introduction

In Chapters one and two, Related Literature on International/Overseas Students' Experience were reviewed. The objective of chapter three is to present and analyse the findings of this research.

This chapter reports the findings of the survey of the academic, personal and social experiences of International/Overseas Students. It also investigates sources of assistance to them as well as factors that create barriers in the assistance they receive from counsellors in Institutions of Higher Education (HE). Discussion of the findings will be presented, while the counsellors' and staff views of what constitutes overseas students' problems and barriers in working with overseas students will be presented and discussed in subsequent publications.

3.2. Background Information

Questionnaires were distributed to Twelve Institutions of Higher Learning in England, Scotland and Wales. The survey was conducted in the 1994/1995 academic sessions. Further group and individual interviews were conducted in 1995/96 session. Two hundred and fifty questionnaires were distributed and two hundred and four were returned. Two were not valid because they were completed by students outside the regions of the research field. Two hundred and two were valid, giving an 80.8% return rate.

The findings of this survey will be analysed against the background of the national profile of overseas students for the same period 1994/1995. The

Higher Education Statistics Agency (HESA) produces periodic data on the characteristics of students in UK higher education (HE). **The HESA report will be incorporated in this presentation.** The findings of this study will also be compared with the findings of some surveys carried out in the 1990s on the experiences of overseas students.

3.3 Data Presentation

HESA's report of July 1995 showed that there were over one and half million enrolments on higher education courses at higher education institutions in the UK. One in ten of these students were from overseas. The same report shows that there are 180 higher education institutions of which around 100 are universities.

The findings of this survey are presented in the same sequence as the questions were asked in the questionnaire that is, using the questionnaire structure as an analytic framework.

3.4 The Institutions covered in this research

The survey was carried out in ten universities and two theological institutions in the UK. The sample was selected to represent a cross-section of different types and locations. For reasons of confidentiality the institutions are referred to by numbers and locations rather than by names.

Six were established universities (over 50 years of existence), two were new (less than forty years). Two were former polytechnics and two were theological colleges.

According to HESA 1995 report, there are 100 universities in the UK so the research sample of 10 universities represents 10% of the national profile.

The institutions were located in Scotland, Wales, The Midlands, The South-east and London. HESA indicates that the majority of students attend institutions in England and so the sample conforms roughly to the national profile.

Section A
This section contains basic information about the students and covers questions 1-9 of the questionnaire

3.5 Academic status
Table one, shows the academic status of participants.

Table 1 Academic Status

Academic Status	No	%
Undergraduate	82	40.6
Postgraduate	120	59.4
Total	202	100

Of the respondents 40.6% (82) are undergraduates while 59.4% (120) are postgraduates. The sample has more postgraduates than undergraduates which conforms to the national data for, according to HESA 1995:15, 'Overseas students comprise 32% of full-time postgraduate and 9% of full-time undergraduates.' This shows that there are more overseas postgraduate students than undergraduates.

3.6. Country of Origin

Tables 2 to 5 show countries of origin of respondents. Through purposive sampling methods (see methodology chapter 2) students were selected from countries from non-western regions, viz. Asia, Africa, Latin America and the Middle East.

50% (99) are from Asian region, 40% (80) from African region 5% (9) from Latin America and 6% (14) are from Middle-East (including Greek and Turkey) regions. Overseas students from Greece and Turkey had asked to be included in Middle-East region because they say they have cultural and religious affinity with this region rather than with the European Community (EC).

Of all students of the Asian region Malaysian students are the highest 54% (27). In the national data Malaysia tops the list of 'the top twenty non-EC domiciles'. The research sample also corresponds with the national data as 14 out of the 20 are countries sampled in this research. The other countries include: Hong Kong, Singapore, Japan, China, Cyprus, Taiwan, India, Turkey, Pakistan, Kenya, Iran, Nigeria, and Thailand. The sample represents 70% of the proportion of overseas students by region of the world studying in the UK. These countries, especially, Malaysia, Singapore and Hong Kong have had a long tradition of sending students to the UK and account for a large proportion of the international students studying in UK. The sample also includes students from countries emerging as international market growth areas, such as Indonesia and Thailand.

Table 2 Country of Origin - Asian Region

Asian Region	No	%
Malaysia	27	13.4
Singapore	8	3.96
Hong Kong	9	4.45
China	9	4.45
India	12	5.94
North Korea	4	1.98
South Korea	2	0.99
Indonesia	4	1.98
Japan	3	1.48
Philippines	3	1.48
Sri Lanka	3	1.48
Taiwan	4	1.98
Thailand	7	3.46
Bangladesh	2	0.99
Pakistan	1	0.49
Brunei	1	0.49
Total No from Asian region		
	99	

Table 3 Country of Origin - African Region

African Region	No	%
Ghana	11	5.44
Kenya	11	5.44
Nigeria	20	9.9
Malawi	2	0.99
Sierraleone	2	0.99
Zambia	5	2.47
Zaire	1	0.49
S. Africa	1	0.49
Ivory Coast	1	0.49
Eritrea	1	0.49
Tanzania	5	2.47
Madagasca	1	0.49
Botswana	7	3.46
Bhutan	1	0.49
Uganda	1	0.49
Zimbabwe	3	1.48
Guyana	2	0.99
Gambia	2	0.99
Togo	1	0.49
Sudan	2	0.99
Total	80	

Table 4 Country of Origin - Latin America & Caribbean Regions

Latin American & Car	No	%
Carribean Islands		
Brazil	2	0.99
Dominican Islands	1	0.49
Mexico	1	0.49
Bahamas	2	0.99
Montser	1	0.49
Venezuela	1	0.49
Argentina	1	0.49
Total	9	

Table 5 Country of Origin - Middle East with Greece & Turkey

Middle East with Greece & Turkey	No	%
Saudi	2	0.99
Bahrain	1	0.49
Greece	3	1.48
Iran	1	0.49
Turkey	4	1.98
Lebanon	1	0.49
Cyprus	2	0.99
Total	14	

HESA Data Report 1994/95

Students in Higher Education

"Top twenty" non-EC domiciles

Country	Thousands
1. Malaysia	13.7
2. Hong Kong	9.8
3. United States of America	7.3
4. Singapore	6.0
5. Japan	3.1
6. Norway	2.3
7. P.R. China	2.3
8. Cyprus	2.2
9. Canada	2.2
10. Taiwan	1.9
11. Israel	1.7
12. India	1.6
13. Turkey	1.6
14. Pakistan	1.5

15. Kenya	1.4
16. Iran	1.1
17. Nigeria	1.1
18. Thailand	1.1
19. Sweden	1.0
20. Australia	1.0

This research sample covers (70%) 14 out of 20 of the "Top Twenty Countries from which overseas students in UK higher education originate (HESA data above). The others Norway, Israel, Canada, Sweden and Australia are outside the scope of this study.

On the basis of the above this sample could lay a modest claim to being representative and the findings generalisable, but the main aim of this study, as has been explained in chapter 2 on methodology is not on generalisation but extrapolation.

3.7. Gender

Table 6 represents the gender profile of respondents. 70% (142) of the sample were male while 30% (60) were female. This is in line with the national profile which records that there were more male than female overseas students studying in UK higher education institutions. (Allen & Higgins 1994)

Table 6 Gender

Gender	No	%
Male	142	70.3
Female	60	29.7
Total	202	100

3.8. Age Range

Table 7 represents the age range of respondents. The highest number of respondents 57% (115) fall into the 21-30 range, while 30% (61) were in the 31-40 age range. In the national profile HESA report shows that '42% of overseas domiciled undergraduates, compared to just 14% of UK domiciled undergraduates were aged between 21 and 24 years on entry' (HESA 1995:15).

Table 7. Age Range

Age Range	No	%
Under 20	10	5
21-30	115	57
31-40	61	30
41 and over	16	8
Total	202	100

3.9. Marital Status

Table 8 shows that there were more single 56.9% (115) respondents than married 42.1% (85) ones.

Out of the numbers that are married, 48 only said their spouses were with them in the UK (Table 9). This of course is relevant to the question of loneliness and homesickness already mentioned.

Table 8 Marital Status

Marrital Status	No	%
Single	115	56.9
Married	85	42.1
Divorced	2	1
Seperated	0	0
Widowed	0	0
Total	202	100

Table 9 Spouse in the UK

Spouse in the UK	No	%
Not applicable	119	59%
Yes	48	23.8
NO	35	17.3
Total	202	100

3.10. Course of Study

Table 10 shows the courses being studied by respondents. The highest number of university overseas' students (15.8%) were studying Engineering, followed by Business/Management (10.8%). This is in line with HESA 1995:16 report which states that "Overall the subject area with the highest proportion of overseas students is: Engineering & Technology where 19% of all students are domiciled outside the UK". Further explanations are given as:

- The courses with the highest proportion of overseas students are those which are perceived as career-oriented: Engineering & Technology, Law and Business & Administrative Studies.
- The subject at postgraduate level having the largest number of overseas students is Business & Administrative Studies.
- The subject at undergraduate level having the largest number of overseas students is Engineering & Technology.

The report further shows that Veterinary Science has the lowest number of students from other countries. This compares positively with the findings of this study because Veterinary Science (0.99%) and Fine Art (0.49%) have the lowest number of overseas students.

These findings show that the highest proportions of overseas students are in courses that are perceived as career-oriented are connected with the areas of need in their home countries. As most come from developing countries they are often sponsored by the government or organisations to study in the UK and return home to assist in the development of their country in related ways. This can perhaps throw some light on the levels of pressure to succeed and to return home or to meet their sponsors completion target which overseas students' experience and which they have also indicated in this study.

It also seems interesting that overseas students hardly study Veterinary Medicine because most Governments and organisations will not sponsor students to study Veterinary Medicine abroad because the few who are needed in life-stock industries are trained locally. Moreover in most developing countries individuals do not keep pets in the same proportion as in the UK and some other Western countries.

Table 10 Course of Study

Course of study	No	%
Engineering	32	15.8
Law	8	3.9
Business Studies etc	22	10.89
Medicine & Nursing	7	3.46
Agriculture & Forestry	19	9.4
Chemistry, Geol & Biol Sciences	19	9.4
Sociology & Human Studies	9	4.45
Education	4	1.98
Research	14	6.93
Public Health & Nutrition	6	2.97
Sports, & Tourism	6	2.97
Vet Medicine	2	0.99
Commun. & Information Syst.	3	1.48
Real Estate, Survey & Construct	8	3.96
Hotel Management, etc	7	3.46
Mathematics	3	1.48
Fine Art	1	0.49
Theology	25	12.37
Total	202	

Ten Top Courses of study in National Profile (HESA data)

The ten top courses of study in the National profile are: Engineering, Business/Management, Social sciences, Accountancy, Maths/computing/Physical Sciences, Medicine/Biological Sciences, Law, Art & Design, Humanities (HESA 1995). Allen & Higgins 1994 and Ames 1996 mention Languages as an area also attracting overseas students.

3.11 Length of stay in the Institution

Table 11 shows that 78% (158) of the respondents had spent under two years by the time of the survey. 15% (30) had spent 2-3 years while the rest had spent three years and over.

Table 11 Length of stay in Institution

Length of Stay in Institution	No	%
Under 2 years	158	78.2
2-3 years	30	14.85
3-4 years	5	2.47
4 years & over	9	4.45
Total	202	

3.12 Length of stay in the UK

Table 12 shows that 40.6% of respondents had spent 1-2 years in the UK, while 29.7% had spent under 1 year. The others had been in the UK for three years and over.

Table 12

Length of Stay in the UK	No	%
Under 1 year	60	29.7
1-2 years	82	40.6
3-4 years	34	16.8
Over 4 years	26	12.9
Total	202	

SECTION B

In this section respondents were asked to indicate needs and problems they had experienced in studying in the UK. They were given a list (compiled from the interviews) and asked which problems they experienced at the beginning of their studies (Initial problems) and which were the problems they were experiencing at present (current problems). They were also asked to indicate those that were never a problem. These were divided into sub-sections A-D. These are presented here following the order in the questionnaire.

The question asked was (no.10) 'The following is a sample of problems students face while studying in a foreign country. Which of these, if any, did you experience at the beginning of your studies and which do you still experience now?' The responses are presented under the questionnaire subheadings below. (Percentages approximated to the nearest whole number). *No response was regarded as 'Never was a problem'*

3.13. Adjustment and Accommodation Issues

Table13. In this section Adjusting to a different culture 46% (92), Getting adequate accommodation 39% (79) and Homesickness 34% (67) were the most frequently mentioned problems. When asked which of the problems were current concerns, Homesickness 32% (64), Loneliness 26% (54) and Cultural adjustment 22% (44) were the top three.

This is similar to the findings of the survey by Allan & Higgins (1994) which rate 'Finding suitable accommodation' as (45%), and another survey which rates it as 42% (Ames 1996). Other problems reported by correspondents in these two surveys as potential problems are: academic problem 44% and the weather 42%. Mixing with students (42%), the weather (41%) and academic problems (41%) were the most frequently mentioned initial problems.

One major difference between this study and HEIST research is the issue of adjustment to UK culture. This is rated 45% in this study but rated 26% in the HEIST research by Allen and Higgins.

Table 13 Adjustment and Accommodation

Adjustment and Accommodation	Never was a problem	%	Was a problem	%	Still is a problem	%
Getting adequate accomodation	99	49	79	39.1	24	11.9
Cultural adjustment	66	32.6	92	45.5	44	21.8
Isolation	98	48.5	63	31.2	41	20.3
Lonliness	91	4.5	57	28.2	54	26.7
Homesickness	69	34.1	67	33.7	64	31.7

3.14. Academic Issues

Table 14 shows that for 39% (79) of the respondents Assignment writing was an initial problem. Followed by: Difficulty in using the computer 34% (68), Different study method 31% (62). Pressure to perform well 48% (96) and Language difficulties 25% (51) are the two currently occurring concerns. Some issues diminish in relative concern over time e.g. Getting information and the Use of computer, while Pressure to perform well increases over time.

Table 14 Academic Issues

Academic Academic Issues	Never was a problem	%	Was a problem	%	Still is a problem	%
Assignment writing	74	36.6	79	39.1	49	24.2
Getting low marks	115	56.9	40	19.8	47	23.2
Pressure to perform well	70	34.7	36	17.8	96	47.5
Language difficulties	96	47.5	55	27.2	51	25.2
Different study method	109	54	62	30.7	31	15.3
Obtaining relevant information	100	49.5	55	27.2	47	23.2
Using the computer	87	43	68	33.7	47	23.2

3.15. C Family, Food and Health

Table15. In this section respondents said the Weather 28% (56) and not finding familiar food items 26% (52) were problems. However what they perceive as current problems are the high cost of making contact with family 56% (114), and the Weather 40% (80). The low concern over child-care issue can be explained by the proportion of single overseas students in the sample (115).

Table 15 Family, Food and Health

Family, Food & Health	Never was a problem	%	Was a problem	%	Still is a problem	%
Adequate child care	175	86.6	20	9.9	7	3.5
Raising chindren in diff culture	171	84.7	13	6.4	18	8.9
Finding familiar food items	109	54	52	25.7	41	20.3
Expensive to contact family	57	28.2	31	15.3	114	56.4
Falling ill often	160	79.2	32	15.8	10	5
Financial problems	110	49.5	33	16.3	59	29.2
The weather	66	32.7	56	27.7	80	39.6

3.16 Socio-psychological Problems

Table 16 Respondents have indicated not having close friends 32% (65) as one of the initial problems they experienced. The problems they were currently experiencing are racial discrimination, 31% (63) Cold attitude from people 29% (59) and Coping with stereotypes of overseas students

26% (59). Some problems seem to get worse over time e.g. Racial prejudice 13% to 31%, (perhaps because the students become more aware of them) while some problems seem to be of less concern over time e.g. Not having close friends 32% to 19% (possibly because students have found a cohesive cultural group).

Table 16 Socio-psychological Problems

Socio-pychological problems	Never was a problem	%	Was a problem	%	Still is a problem	%
Racial prejudice	112	55.4	27	13.4	63	31.1
Discrimination	126	62.4	25	12.4	51	25.2
Not having close friends	99	49	65	32.2	38	18.8
Lack of self esteem	136	67.3	42	20.8	24	11.9
Coping with Stereotypypes of IS	110	49.5	39	19.3	53	26.2
Security problems	148	73.3	26	12.9	28	13.9
Cold attitude from people	94	46.5	49	24.3	59	29.2
Actions misunderstood	128	63.4	40	19.8	34	16.8

3.17. E. Any Other Problems not included on the list

Comments from open-ended questions are all listed below under academic, personal and social problems. These are reported additional problems and the number of times they appeared are indicated in bracket.

Academic (x1)
Not receiving enough attention from tutors.

Personal (x5)
Not being able to go home for things like funerals of relations.
Generally low in spirit.
Getting good church.
Lack of people you can trust with confidential and personal issues.
Getting extra income through part-time work.

Social (x3)
Not making friends with home students.
Superficial relationship, society and people not open.
Not much to do outside studying.

3.18 Coping Strategies
When asked (Q11) 'What methods, resources or ways did you use/still use to overcome or cope with difficulties?' the comments from open-ended questions were:

Academic strategies (x5)

Study hard.
Consulting lecturers and supervisors on what they require before answering any research paper, instead of just interpreting questions on my own.
I joined a language class and read the leaflets provided by the institution to give information.
Discussion with classmates.
Reserved books in the library as there are usually not enough to go round.

Personal (x5)
Endurance with the aim of achieving the goal am here for.
Reliance on God, through faith and prayers.
My wife and the church I attend have been wonderful resources.
Getting a part-time job.
Indifference and an inner ability to survive.

Social (x9)
Spending time with fellow-nationals.

Made a lot of friends through sports.
Learning to look at things from local's point of view.
Adapting to life in the UK.
Taking initiative to be friendly and socialise.
I was observant, took time to understand the society, culture and people. This has greatly helped me.
Writing e-mail to friends and family and sharing problems with them.
Being aware that I am in another country with its own idiosyncrasies
Associating with people from other foreign countries and helping each other.

3.19. From whom respondents seek support or help.

Table17. When asked: From whom did you seek support or assistance? 70% (141) said **Friends** followed by Personal tutor 58% (118) and Other overseas students 42% (85). This finding is similar to that of Allan and Higgins (1994) and Ames (1996) who report that their respondents said 'Friends would be my first choice'. They noted a lack of interest in consulting institution's counsellors/advisers.

According to a study of the experience of students in higher education (Roberts and Higgins (1992), the resistance to discussing problems with advisers/counsellors is also evident among UK students. Some felt that approaching a counsellor/adviser was an admission of failure, while others felt like many overseas students that they could not approach someone they did not know.

Table 17. Sources of Support

Sources of support	No	%
Personal tutor	118	58.42
Counsellor	15	7.43
Chaplain	16	7.92
Hall warden	15	7.43
Accomodation officer	21	10.4
Student union	31	15.35
Welfare officer	12	5.94
International student officer	19	9.41
Other overseas students	85	42.08
Home students	54	26.73
Religious organizations	23	11.39
Friends	141	69.8
Others.	24	11.88

3.20 How helpful were they?

When asked 'How helpful are they?' Respondents placed the names of those who were helpful under: very helpful, helpful and not helpful, as follows.

'Very helpful' were Friends and Other overseas students and Personal tutors.

'Helpful' in different circumstances were Student Union, Accommodation officers, Home students, Religious organisations.

CHAPTER FOUR
DISCUSSIONS OF THE FINDINGS OF
INTERNATIONAL/OVERSEAS STUDENTS' EXPERIENCE.

4.1. Introduction

In the previous chapter the findings of the surveys and interviews of overseas student's academic, personal, social and cultural experiences were presented. This chapter discusses the findings in the light of their implications for overseas students' adaptation and adjustment to living and studying in the UK.

4.2. Adjustment Problems

As the findings show, the main areas of concern to students in this study under adjustment and accommodation issues are 'Homesickness' 34% (67), 'Loneliness and Adjustment to a different culture' 46% (92). Homesickness and loneliness seem to be experienced by most people who move away from home. According to Furnham (1997) the key features of homesickness appear to be a strong preoccupation with thoughts of home, a perceived need to go home, a sense of grief for the home and a concurrent feeling of unhappiness, unease and disorientation in the new place which is not home.

Adjustment to a new culture was also reported by overseas students as a concern because they feel like strangers and have difficulty knowing the acceptable ways of doing thinks in the UK. According to Van Deurzen-Smith (1996) being a stranger is to be alienated and it gives you a sinking feeling of no longer having any point of reference.

Overseas students are people in transition who have come to accomplish an educational goal with a view to returning home. They come with high expectations based on pre-arrival packages they receive which though colourful are seen by many as unrealistic. Furnham (1997) argues that the more accurate, objective and comprehensive a sojourner's expectations of the new society are, the more successful the adaptation process becomes. High expectations that are not fulfilled by institutions are said to be related to poor adjustment. This implies that institutions should give as accurate a picture of the institution and society in the pre-arrival package as possible.

Moving to a different country to study often involves leaving behind family, friends, colleagues, and neighbours; as a result sources of social support are reduced and there is often an increase in homesickness and stress. Overseas students should be encouraged and assisted to form new social support and friendship networks to help to reduce the effect of homesickness.

4.3. Academic Issues

As the data show, the problems some overseas students experience in the initial stages of their studies include 'Assignment writing and Use of the computer' 39% (79). These can be summed up under problems associated with moving from one academic system to another. Most overseas students say they come from academic systems that differ from the UK system in many ways, e.g. in methods of assessment, which create expectations in the learners as to what the assessors want in order to get a pass grade. There is also the difficulty of moving from a dependent learning system to an independent self-motivated system. Some overseas students say they come from systems where interactive learning is not often practised. In their system the lecturers are venerated as all-knowing and it is difficult for some students to adapt to the UK system where they are encouraged to enter into debates with their lecturers.

The implications are that assisting students to learn to express disagreement and to interact in class is essential. Those overseas students should be given clear guidelines when they are asked to make a presentation. Students should be encouraged to ask for an explanation of essay or project titles.

'The use of English as a second or foreign language' is another area of concern for overseas students according to the findings. Foreign language users, e.g. students from Middle East and Latin America, learned English as an academic subject while second-language users like most students from the Commonwealth countries have used English as a medium of education. For both groups use of language which is inappropriate because they are not fully aware of social conventions may create frontiers and alienate them. Some have indicated their difficulty in articulating their thoughts and feelings in a foreign language while others said in interviews that lack of skills to express themselves adequately in a second language has cost them marks. Difficulty in marketing their knowledge as much as possible has meant that members of staff often do not understand what they want to say and mark them on what staff think the students are saying. According to Van Deurzen - Smith (1996:3):

When we give up our mother tongue for another language we are truly disabled and bereft. The initial struggle to acquire another language to a decent level of fluency is humiliating enough in itself. You find yourself babbling like a baby and unable to express the complex thoughts that used to flow from you so easily when you put them into what seemed like naturally available words.

She went on to say that you have to rack your brain and the words still won't come and what is worse is that other people judge your mental abilities by the sounds you make.

Elton (1985) argues that reading presents the least difficulties but adequate and suitable styles are often problems in students' written

English. Overseas students should therefore politely ask staff to explain what they do not understand e.g. slang, acronyms and complex figures of speech.

'Pressure to perform well' 48% (96) and to meet sponsor's and family's expectations and deadline are all factors that cause concern to some overseas students according to the findings in this section. This pressure was not widely recognised and in some cases remained unnoticed by academic and support services staff within campuses, according to students interviewed. There is therefore need to assist students to work within their time schedules recognising the importance of pressures which arise from outside the academic institution.

4.4. Family, Food and Health

The findings show that for some overseas students the initial problems were 'The weather' 28% (56) and 'Finding familiar food items', 26% (52) while current difficulties were still 'The weather' 40% (80) and 'High cost of contacting family' 56% (114). To be able to contact home cheaply is an important need of overseas students which is not easily noticed by institutions and those working with students. Surface mail to some of their countries is unreliable and some letters take a very long time to arrive at their destinations. Most students rely on the telephone where possible but these are extremely expensive costing up to £3 or more for three minutes! (There is a significant difference between this and the 20p or so it costs a home student to reach parents and family anywhere in the UK for the same length of time).

I am glad to add here that in recent years communication to family and friends have improved drastically with the introduction of the internet and mobile phones. Communication as it is now is in no way what it was at the time of the survey, and this is a good thing.

For some students finding familiar food items is a problem. According to Van Deurzen-Smith (1996) it is remarkable to find that a large part of one's sense of security and identity is based on such simple things as food items one is used to. Overseas students should be directed to where to buy food items from their regions. Continuing students can assist new ones to locate special shops that stock such food items. The student union can also help in organising such assistance.

Another great improvement in the international students' experience from the time of the survey is that food items from different parts of the world are much more available now, which is very good.

4.5. Social & psychological problems

Findings in this section show that some respondents have indicated 'Not having close friends' 32% (65) as one of the initial problems they experienced. The current problems in this section include 'Racial discrimination' 31% (63) and 'Coping with stereotypes of overseas students' 26% (53).

A small number of students reported that they had experienced racial prejudice in some form or another. Some reported not having close friends as an initial problem because they found home students unfriendly. It is significant that this ceases to be a major problem once they are able to make friends among other overseas students, especially from their home country. They also had to cope with staff and home students' negative stereotype conception of overseas students. They found that most home students had minimal knowledge of overseas countries, and the little they know seems to be based on negative media images of non-western countries.

4.6. Other problems

Other areas of concern reported by students are: Personal issues (x5) e.g. 'Not able to go home for family functions such as funerals and weddings', 'Academic issues' (x1) e.g. 'Not getting enough attention from tutors' and 'Financial issues' (x1) 'Not getting part-time jobs to improve their financial status'.

Overseas students say they go through considerable emotional strain because of their inability to go home when they lose a close family member especially a parent. Some are unable to concentrate on their studies. Some students disclosed that they were not receiving enough attention from their tutors, and had no way of bringing this to the knowledge of the authorities because of fear of victimisation. Institutions should set up a departmental staff/student support groups where students would feel free to discuss their concerns without fear of repercussions.

The need for part-time jobs to help overseas students who need some financial assistance is of some concern to some students. During the interviews students said they underestimated the amount they needed for maintenance. Examples given include the expense on winter clothing as most of them have come from tropical countries and could not imagine the severity of the cold months. Many thought they needed only a couple of cardigans but discovered that they needed to buy heavy and expensive winter coats. The private students were the most affected. Some said that finding the thousands of pounds for their fees meant that they had very little money left for their personal needs. Some came with the hope of getting some part-time work to help to maintain a healthy financial balance.

The implication is that institutions need to make some allowances for students to get part-time work on or off the campus. Freeing students' minds from financial worries will enable them to concentrate for most of their time on their academic work.

Overseas Students' Coping Strategies

Participants in this study have devised their own coping strategies which include the following:

4.7. Social and personal strategies

Under this section responses were: 'Spending time with fellow nationals', 'Making friends through sports', and 'Learning to look at things from the locals points of view'. 'Writing e-mail to friends', 'Endurance and a conscious effort of focusing on achieving the goal they are here for' for a good number, 'Reliance on God through faith and prayers'.

It is significant that 'Spending time with fellow nationals' is a coping strategy most overseas students find beneficial. Furnham (1997) argues that there is available evidence in literature regarding the supportive functions of interpersonal relationships to suggest that social support is directly related to increased speed and quality of adaptation as well as breaking the clear links between stress and illness. Also that the various types of support provided by interpersonal relationships play a crucial role in determining a person's general adaptive functioning and sense of well-being.

'Learning to look at things from the locals' point of view' is a method of adjusting to their new environment by some overseas students. According to Van Deurzen-Smith (1996) one discovers new sides to the same old questions through moving to a different country and finding one's usual assumptions undermined and contradicted. This enables one not to take sides, but to view things from a variety of positions and to review one's own opinions, mitigating them with new input. She further argues that such flexibility of perspective is an essential asset for life in the world of tomorrow where people from different nations will have to get on with each other in ever closer co-operation in a shrinking world.

'Reliance on God through faith and prayers' as a strategy for some overseas students points to the importance of the issue of beliefs for overseas students. Higher education institutions are multi-faith environments and students' religion or lack of it will have some bearing on their behaviour and their values. Overseas students come from various religious backgrounds and there are varying degrees of commitment to an individual faith. Members of the same faith will also have different levels of devoutness.

In particular, some religions have a different status for males and females which has implications for assigning supervisors of the opposite sex; some religions do not allow their females to shake hands with males. Some religions have dietary regulations which may have implications for departmental social activities.

The implications are that taking account of religious beliefs can be very difficult. Awareness, sensitivity and discussion can prevent embarrassment and misunderstanding. According to the interview findings, (Christian Theological students and Turkish Muslim students) overseas students are normally happy and willing to discuss religious matters, and often find it difficult to understand the taboo placed on religion as a topic of social interaction in the UK.

4.8. Academic strategies

'Consulting lecturers and supervisors on what they require before doing an assignment' and 'Discussion with classmates' are two of the strategies used by overseas students according to the responses. It would be helpful for members of staff to be explicit about what they require in any assignment, project or piece of work they ask their students to carry out and they should check that the students understand.

4.9. Overseas Students' Sources of Support

The research findings show that respondents say their sources of support are 'Friends 70% (141), 'Personal tutors' 58% (118) and 'Other overseas students' 42% (85). They said in interviews that they turned to 'friends' especially their fellow nationals for help because these students understood and appreciated what they were experiencing having been through the problems themselves. Other sources of support are personal tutors and other overseas students. The interview findings show that, although the second highest percentage said they consulted their personal tutors, yet in terms of the actual help received it was their friends (highest percentage) who gave the needed support. These friends have been described as 'Caring and understanding friends who have had similar problems'.

4.9. These findings highlight two implications:

First, the role of <u>Personal tutors.</u> Although not the focus of this study, this observation deserves mention here in view of its high rating in the frequency table of this study (3.2). There is a mismatch in tutor-student expectations. These findings corroborate Klopper (1991) findings regarding the difference in student/tutor role expectation. Consequently she suggested that institutions should (a) consider the policy of selecting tutors for overseas students (b) define the principal functions of the academic tutor, bearing in mind the potential additional support overseas students may expect, (c) include the discussion of expectations and roles in initial meetings of tutors and overseas students and (d) make available a handbook for all tutors working with overseas students. (See also Okorocha (1982))

<u>Peer-counselling</u>. Evidence from the findings of this study is that students receive the most help and assistance from their friends. This supports previous studies. (Idowu 1985; Okorocha 1990; Al-Shawi 1990 and Klopper 1991.)

Furthermore, Pedersen (1975) in his review of research data from 781 students of University of Minnesota said that for overseas students, the most sought source of help for solving personal problems was a fellow national. He concluded that this was because co-nationals are readily available and in most cases more acceptable. Similarly, Idowu (1985) shows that African students seek help from peers or other sources and argues that the low percentage of contact with the counselling centres ought to pose concern to college counsellors.

Pedersen (1991) sees this as a challenge that can be utilised in the right direction by training overseas students as peer-counsellors. He points out, though, that this has had limited success because the informal network of peers is difficult to identify. Also quite often the sought-out peers are not interested in being trained. He concludes by saying that the concept of peer-counselling, nonetheless, affords another way of providing counselling to overseas students, although more work is needed in developing this model.

CHAPTER FIVE
COUNSELLING SERVICE

5.1. International/Overseas Students' Views of Counselling Service

Table18. The counselling service is one of the support services that most institutions provide for all students. When asked in (Q.13) 'Does your university/institution have a student counselling service?' A high proportion of respondents 76% (153) said Yes, a small proportion 3% (6) said No but a rather substantial percentage 21% (43) said they were Not Aware that their institution provided such services. These responses point to the issue of publicity of services and the provision of adequate information which have been discussed earlier.

Table 18 Counselling Service in Institution

Counselling service in Institution	No	%
Yes	153	75.7
No	6	3
Not aware	43	21.3
Total	202	

5.2. Visiting the counsellor with problems

Table19. When asked in (Q 14a) 'If you have experienced some difficulties, have you been to see a counsellor?' 50% (100) said 'No'; 18% (37) said 'Yes' while 32% (65) said the Services were never Required. This was also reported in Roger and Smith (1992) research which referred to lack of interest in consulting institution's counsellors.

Table 19 Visited a Counsellor?

Have you been to see a counsellor for assistance	No	%
Yes	37	18.3
No	100	49.5
Never required	65	32.1
Total	202	

5.3. Reasons for not seeing a counsellor

Q14a asked 'If you have experienced some difficulties, have you been to see a counsellor?' Those who have experienced some difficulties but did not go to a counsellor for assistance gave the following reasons which fall under personal, cultural, social, nature of service and counselling outcome.

Personal (x3)
Do not like to share personal problems with a stranger.
Do not know him/her well enough.
I see a problem as a challenge for me to solve it myself.

Cultural (x4)
They are all whites.
They are not easily available and I see cultural barriers.
Not easily accessible.
I am not familiar with professional counselling system. I share problems with friends - people I know.

Nature of service and outcome of counselling (x 5)
They would not solve any of my problems.
Lack of confidentiality
Think it would be a waste of time, polite smiles but no genuine action.

They seemed too distant.
Not sure where they are and how they can help.

5.4. What kind of problems would you have taken to a counsellor

Q14 asked 'If 'no' what kind of problems would you have taken to a counsellor?' The following is a list of problems respondents said they would have taken to a counsellor 'if' they had been to see one:

Academic progress (x3)
Assignment and exam stress.
Study difficulties.
Lack of concentration.

Personal (x7)
Emotional problems and loneliness.
Personal and financial.
How to cope with inferiority and how to get my family over which has failed and is very painful.
Shortage of funds.
Depression.
Coping with homesickness
How to boost my self-esteem.

Social (x4)
Racial discrimination to see how she/he can help to overcome it.
Family, friendship and social life.
Special problem needing professional help.
Relationship progress.

5.5. Problems actually taken to a counsellor by a few students

Q.14d asked 'If 'Yes' to Q14a what kind of problems did you take to a counsellor?'

The problems respondents who had been to see a counsellor reported are similar to those already reported and are under academic, personal and social issues:

Academic (3)
Study issues
Problem relating to my supervisor and work circumstances.
Problems with research

Personal (x2)
Family matters
Finding accommodation for family

Social (x3)
Depression
Accommodation
Poll tax/council tax

5.6. Outcome of visit to a counsellor

Table20. In Q 15 participants were asked 'If you have been to see a counsellor how useful was the help you received?' Table 20 shows that among the few that have been to see a counsellor, 5% (11) found it very useful, 10% (20) found it useful and 5% (11) did not find it useful.

Table 20 How useful was the Assistance?

How useful was the assistance?	No	%
Very useful	11	5.4
Useful	20	9.9
Not useful	11	5.4
Not applicable	160	79.2
Total	202	

5.7 How often did you visit the counsellor?

Table21. Very few respondents had seen a counsellor and of these 8% (17) went once, 7% (15) went more than once while only 2% (4) completed the agreed time contract.

Table21. How often did you visit the counsellor?

How often did you visit the counsellor?		
Response	No	%
Once	17	8.4
A few times	15	7.4
Completed agreed time	4	1.98
Not applicable	166	82.1
Total	202	

5.8. How they decided to visit the counsellor

Table 22. Respondents were asked in Question 17 'How did you decide to go to a counsellor?' Out of the few that had been to a counsellor 9% (18) decided to go on their own, 2% (4) were accompanied by their friends, 4% (8) went because they were referred by their tutor.

Table 22 How did you decide to go?

Response	How did you decide to go to a counsellor? No	%
Referred	8	3.96
Went alone	18	8.9
Accompanied by a friend	4	1.98
Not applicable	162	80
Total	202	

CHAPTER SIX
BARRIERS TO COUNSELLING INTERNATIONAL STUDENTS

6.1. Barriers to the effective help a counsellor could offer respondents

Table23. Q. 18 asked 'To what extent would the following be barriers to the effective help a counsellor could offer you?' Respondents indicated items from the list provided:

1) Issues (Concerns) about the counsellor or the counselling service

Major responses are Guidance is not given in counselling with a high 96% (193). This is followed by Service not helpful 93% (183) and 'The counsellor will not understand me' 82% (165). Others are Not sure of role of counsellor 79% (160), Lack of confidence in the counsellor 77% (155) and Not sure of successful outcome of visit 72% (145).

The implications of these are discussed later. The respondents were also asked about issues that create barriers on their own part and the responses follow:

Table 23 Barriers - Concerns about the Counsellor and Service

Barriers to effective counselling of international of international Students				
Things about the counsellor or counselling service Responses	Yes	%	No	%
Not awear that service exists	152	75.25	50	24.75
Not sure of role/work of the coun sellor	160	79.21	42	20.79
Not sure of successful outcome of visit	145	71.78	57	28.22
Lack of confidence in the counsellor	155	76.73	47	23.27
The counsellor will not understand you	165	81.68	37	18.32
From what you hear the service is not helpful	187	92.58	15	7.43
Guidance is not given in counselling	193	95.54	9	4.46

Issues (concerns) about Yourself (The Overseas Student)

Table24. In this section respondents were asked to what extent the issues (relating to them as overseas students) in the list supplied would be barriers to the effective help a counsellor could offer them. The responses were 'Cannot afford the time' 85% (171) 'Religious belief' 83% (168), 'Stigma attached to seeking professional help' 82% (166) and 'Counselling will imply invasion of privacy' 81% (164). Others are 'Language difficulties 78% (157), 'Would rather rely on people of same culture' 68% (137) and Cultural differences will hinder the help received 67% (136).

Table 24 Barriers - Concerns about Self (Overseas students)

Things about yourself (The international student) Responses	Yes	%	No	%
Cultural differences will hinder the help received	136	67.33	66	32.67
Religious beliefs	168	83.17	34	16.83
Language difficulties	157	77.72	45	22.27
Stigma attached to seeking professional help	166	82.18	36	17.82
Counselling will imply invasion of privacy	164	81.19	38	18.81
Would rather rely on people of same culture	137	67.82	65	32.18
Can not afford the time	171	84.65	31	15.35

6.2. Other things that might discourage overseas students from going to see a counsellor.

Question 19 asked 'What else does or might discourage you from going to see a counsellor? Comments from open-ended questions were similar to those respondents gave as reasons for not going to see a counsellor and fall under the same categories of personal, cultural, nature of service and outcome of counselling and social issues.

Personal (x5)
I believe in counselling myself.

I am a very private person who does not disclose personal problems to a stranger.
Language problems.
Tutors, faculty staff, classmates and friends are good enough to help with all difficulties.
Counsellors might suggest actions or methods which I may disagree or object to.

Cultural (x3)
The counsel may not be culturally relevant. The fact that in the interaction with overseas students, counsellors often do not appreciate the cultural difference. This may result in a total misunderstanding of students' problems.
Counsellor will not understand problem from my point of view.

6.3. Nature of service and outcome of counselling (x14)
Not many people can easily be talked to.
It is all routine, seem to have the same attitude to foreign students - have heard the problem before.
Find the exercise very demanding.
Too professional.
The time it would take to complete a particular course of programme.
Low expectation.
Confidentiality.
Not solving a specific problem after counselling.
Accessibility of offer.
They seem too distant.
Leaking the preceding of the counselling session (Telling others about the discussion)
Most of my problems remain unsolved, can't wait to get back home.
It is not easy to walk into a stranger's office for counselling. It is easier if a prior acquaintance has been established.

Social (x4)
I do not like the idea because they are whites.
Racial discrimination.

Prejudice about the counsellor (Students' prejudice about counsellor).
Being embarrassed if someone else finds out e.g. English friend.

6.4. Persons who have helped international students most in solving their problems.

Respondents were asked (Q20)' Who has helped you most in solving your problems? (state in order of helpfulness).' The following responses were given. This reinforces the earlier question on 'whom overseas students seek support from'. This is a questioning approach where you ask respondents similar questions and see if there is a consistency in their answers. Here the emphasis is that overseas students seek help from a variety of people depending on the problem but the greatest resource are **Friends** especially those from the same **nationality**.

6.5. Friends (x 46)

Out of 113 responses 41% (46) said friends especially those from same nationality and other overseas students. Examples of these forty six responses were:
A few friends who are caring and understanding who have had similar problems.
Friends from country of origin.
Overseas students who have been here longer

6.6. Family (x18)

Out of 113 responses 16% (18) said family and typical of these were:
Family through phone call home.
Spouse

6.7. Personal Tutors/staff (x 28)
Personal Tutors and other members of staff were mentioned by 25% (28) of the respondents. Out of these personal tutors were mentioned 18 times while other members of staff including Hall warden, International students' officers and Departmental secretaries were mentioned 10 times.

6.8. Supervisors (x7)
Still under staff, Supervisors were mentioned specifically by 6% (7) of respondents while others were mentioned as follows: Counsellors 2% (2), Doctors 2% (2).

6.9. Religious Beliefs (x 15)
Respondents have indicated their religious belief as a source of support. 13% (15) said the following:
Faith in God.
Christian friends
Chaplain
Church members.

Other Sources mentioned were:
Myself 5% (6), Home students 3 % (3), Sponsors 1% (1).

6.10. Suggestions of ways the counselling service or university can help international students to cope with any difficulties they experience while studying abroad.
The final question in the questionnaire (Q. 21) asked 'Can you suggest any ways your counselling service or university could help overseas

students to cope with any difficulties they experience while studying abroad?'

All the suggestions made are reproduced here and have been put in three categories: Suggestion to the counselling service, to counsellors and to Institution.

Suggestions to counselling service and to counsellors were:

Good orientation for students

Develop ways that encourage overseas students to use the counselling service.

Overseas students would like to make some local friends in order to improve their English, so some social events would help.

Staff and students should gradually establish a relationship.

To understand and appreciate other cultures.

Use of computer network services for those who might want to hide their identity.

*Appointing foreigners too as counsellors or those who have studied abroad themselves.

Being more aware of the difficulties overseas students face.

Show more concern than just counsel - not just a duty. Those who approach them want to feel being accepted rather than feeling like a burden.

Overseas students often need an understanding and friendly person who does not treat them as cases in a file but as persons. This may be difficult but no one likes being handled just as an object. Many counsellors do not have time for this rather they operate from an official distance - maybe out of fear or for their own safety.

6.11. Suggestions to institutions were:

The university should make an effort to settle accommodation problems early as lack of proper accommodation in a strange country and new culture influence the settling down process of individuals.

Have a graduate student from overseas be available to newly arrived students from that particular country.

Good orientation in library, clinic and counselling service.

Staff and students should gradually establish a relationship.

Write guidance book on how to treat foreign students which should inform supervisors and staff.

Being more aware of the difficulties of overseas students.

Need to improve attitude towards overseas students who pay high fees.

Provide part-time jobs to overseas students who need them.

Provide bursary fund to help private overseas students in financial difficulties.

Provide specialist groups for various ethnic groups to help in academic and social difficulties.

Make special effort to recruit some counsellors from overseas people who actually care, people who have had similar experiences.

The authorities should try to overcome (look into) racial discrimination which overseas students experience from some home students and staff.

They should try and see overseas students in the context of their cultural background

*They must have among their staff people of other cultures. This gives one confidence that one is going to be treated as a human being.

There should be more advertising of services available.

Provide regular 'open office' day to introduce counselling and other services.

They should understand the language difficulties experienced by some overseas students for whom English is a 3rd or 4th language, and not expect them to produce the same quality of English expression as the British native speakers.

There is an abysmally poor attitude to overseas students being introduced to the facilities they need for their studies. Sometimes they are left on their own to cope the best they can or 'Discover' the facilities by chance and sometimes they are denied access through prejudice. Universities should realise that these students pay heavily for their studies and come mostly from academically disadvantaged backgrounds. They need a friendly and caring relationship with their supervisors to introduce them early enough to the system.

CHAPTER SEVEN
FINDINGS ON COUNSELLING SERVICES

7.1. Discussion of Findings on Counselling Service.

A high percentage 76% (153) of respondents knew that their institution had a counselling service; some 21% (43) were unaware that their institution provided such a service. This shows the need for more publicity for the activities of the service. It is significant that during an interview with a counsellor in a university in the Midlands, the counsellor admitted that publicity was low but that it was deliberately so. The reason she gave was that they were short-staffed and they would be overwhelmed and unable to cope if they were to have responses to massive publicity.

7.2. Uptake and Non-uptake of counselling by International Students

Only 18% (37) of the participants said they had been to see a counsellor. Approximately 50% (100) had not been to see a counsellor, even when they needed one. And a further 32 % (65) felt they did not require the services. This supports the interview findings from former overseas students and from literature that uptake of counselling among overseas students is low.

Al-Shawi (1990) also found very few of his sample of post-graduate students consulted counsellors at universities about their more serious problems. He observed:

One of the interesting results shows that those who had major problems consulted friends or tutors but not counsellors. (Al-Shawi, 1990:272)

7.3. Reasons for Non-uptake.

Responses fell under the headings Personal (x 5), cultural (x 2), nature of service and outcome of service (x14) and four of these were 'Do not like to share personal problems with a stranger,' 'Don't think they can help in real problems,' 'They are not easily available and I see cultural barriers,' 'They seem too distant'. Others include what the overseas students see as 'lack of interest in people of other cultures', 'bias - they are all whites', 'lack of confidentiality,' 'not easily accessible', 'superficial advice', and the 'unsuccessful outcome of contact'. Others would rather 'rely on family and close friends.'

'Unsuccessful outcome' and 'superficial advice' deserve special mention as they point to overseas students' expectations of counselling and the unsuitability of the counselling approaches used. Idowu (1985) points to the background of some overseas students who go to elders and authority figures for advice and guidance. As a result, most overseas students will enter the counselling situation expecting to receive advice. If such expectation is not satisfied they are not likely to return to see the counsellor. This leads to early termination and subsequently non-uptake of counselling. According to both Exum and Lau and (1988); Esen (1972) the indication is that a structured directive approach would yield greater results than the non-directive approach which most host counsellors tend to use.

Pedersen (1987) argues that a counsellor who adheres strictly to formal western counselling theories will find such an approach unsuitable when helping students from other cultures. He recommends that if counsellors seek to translate counselling to the culturally different, they will need to understand the relative importance of each formal and informal combination of helping alternatives.

It is important that overseas students be treated as individuals during counselling. While some students may prefer a problem-solving directive approach, others who have had a longer interaction with the western culture may prefer a client-centred/non-directive approach.

It is necessary to compare this with the responses of counsellors in the next chapter where they were asked about the approaches they use in counselling overseas students (see 4.2).

7.4. Problems overseas students would/do take to a counsellor

The problems overseas students who have not been to see a counsellor and those who have been said they would and did take to a counsellor are academic issues, accommodation, financial and personal matters; family, psychological and handling of racial discrimination (see 3.2.25). This points to the role expectation of the students in the sample. From the responses they expect the counsellor to be knowledgeable in every area or at least be able to refer students to the right professionals.

This is in line with Al-Shawi's (1990) findings that in a multicultural counselling situation, the counsellor experiences a great variety of alternative roles. These roles - tutor, administrator, instructor etc. - he suggested should not be at variance with the counsellor's role. This is also supported by earlier findings by Idowu (1985) that overseas students rarely come into a helping (counselling) relationship with only one problem. They often come with interrelated problems; therefore, counsellors need to identify the themes of students' concerns in order to put related problems into focus.

Barriers To Effective Counselling of International Students

7.5. Issues (things) about the Counsellor or Service

When overseas students were asked which issues about the counsellor or the service are barriers to effective counselling, the following were the most frequently occurring responses : 'Guidance is not given in counselling' with a high of 95.5%, (193) This is followed by 'Service is not helpful' 93% (187)) and 'The counsellor will not understand me' 81% (165) These reoccur in the open-ended responses and have implications for the approaches used in counselling overseas students.

The credibility of the counsellor working with overseas students is an important precondition for trust and understanding between counsellor and these students as clients. Credibility is based on both expertise and trustworthiness. The multi-cultural counsellor can develop good credibility, when working with overseas students, by learning from their behaviour and being able to integrate the students' world-views without losing his/her own integrity as a culturally influenced person (Sue, 1978).
Such are those Augsburger (1986) describes as culturally aware counsellors who have a capacity for welcoming, entering into, and prizing other world-views without negating their legitimacy. They can enter into the world of others, savour its distinctness, and prize its differences while holding clearly to the uniqueness of their own.

7.6. Issues (things) about the Overseas Students.

Top responses are 'Cannot afford the time' 85% (171), Religious belief 83% (168), 'Stigma attached to seeking professional help' 82% (166) and 'Counselling will imply invasion of privacy' 81% (164).

Respondents think that counselling will take up much of their time. During the interviews some talked of waiting lists in some of the counselling centres. This assertion was also supported by some of the counsellors (4.2) who indicated that because of financial cuts, some institutions are able to employ only part-time counsellors which means large workloads and longer waiting lists.

Some students say they expect guidance to be given in counselling which departs from the western style that emphasises self-help and independence. For some students there is stigma attached to going to see a professional counsellor whose role is often mistaken for that of a psychiatrist. It is necessary for the role of the counsellor to be defined and explained to overseas students.

The effects of Religious beliefs were also highlighted as a form of barrier. A Muslim male student, for instance, will not (willingly) see a female counsellor. A Muslim female student will not shake hands with any male and this creates problems in a situation where a counsellor sees a handshake as a way of welcoming a client and establishing rapport in a counselling situation. The physical location of the counselling service may also have religious implications as some strict Muslims do not use facilities located in premises where alcohol is served. During the exploratory interviews a welfare officer in one of the universities observed that, some strict Muslims who needed the services of the welfare office were reluctant to use it, because the office is located in the Student Union building where alcohol is served. The welfare officer at that point had recommended to the university that the office be moved to another location, so as not to exclude any student from their support service.

Other barriers, not frequently mentioned in this study but linked to religious beliefs, include age and gender. In a multi-cultural counselling relationship, overseas students between the ages of 35 to 45 may have problems relating to younger counsellors, because in some cultures it is only the younger person who goes to an older person for advice and guidance. A female Muslim student will be very reluctant to go to a male counsellor to talk about relationships with the opposite sex.

7.7. The implications of these findings are that students' expectations and their backgrounds e.g. religious beliefs, need to be considered, in order to increase the uptake of counselling among overseas students.

Relevance to overseas students' background
One of the responses in the open-ended sections is 'The counsel may not be culturally relevant' the fear of losing cultural integrity is an anxiety which may influence many overseas students to stay away from counselling centres (Al-Shawi 1990). The ability to join another in his or her culture, while fully owning one's own requires a broadened vision of the task of facilitating human growth and healing according to Augsburger (1986). Counsellors need to consider the importance of cultural behaviour and develop a degree of sensitivity toward it. It is an increasing concern among counsellors and other mental health professionals that cultural variables be given significant consideration in the therapeutic situations to attain effective client outcome (Dillard 1983, Pedersen 1976, Sue 1977).

Dillard (1983) argues that counselling goals be culturally relevant to, and consistent with, the overseas student as an individual as well as his/her culture. Ivey (1971) and Dillard (1983) said that more than 85% of the counselling relationships involve non- verbal communication, which is a significant variable in counselling overseas students.

7.8. How The University or its Counselling Service Could Help.

Overseas students suggested ways the counselling service or the university could help overseas students to cope with any difficulties they experience while studying. All the responses were given in 3.2.32. Some are highlighted below.

7.9. For the counsellors and counselling service (x 10)

Good orientation for students.
Develop ways that encourage overseas students to use the counselling service.
Use of computer network services for those who might want to hide their identity.
 Knowledge of the foreign students' culture and background. This reinforces the need for counsellors' awareness and sensitivity to other cultures.
 Appointing some foreigners as counsellors or those who have studied abroad themselves.

Overseas students suggested that institutions should employ a separate counsellor (who is also a foreigner) for overseas student or have one in the team of support services staff. The issue here is that for such problems as racial discrimination there will be an option for the students to talk to someone they feel will understand them. There are, however, conflicting findings in literature over counsellors' preference. Some are in favour of similar race counsellor, but some give opposite results (Thompson et al 1978). There are preferences for counsellors of similar racial background, there are also preferences based on such matters as gender, age, and having prior information about the counsellor from someone who had experienced counselling. It has been observed that some students tend to prefer a counsellor of the same colour. On the other hand, some students may prefer counsellors who came from a different ethnic group and who had favourable attitudes towards the clients.

The researcher has observed that the preference is usually for counsellors of similar racial and cultural backgrounds when overseas students and clients wish to discuss certain issues like discrimination and prejudice. However in situations where there is a possibility that the counsellor might know their families, overseas students especially Asian young ladies, may prefer to discuss relationship problems with a counsellor of different culture so that the topic of discussion will not inadvertently be passed on to their families in a social context.

7.10 For the institutions (x17)

The university should settle accommodation problems early, ensure good induction and advertise available services.

The University should show that it has a genuine interest in overseas students, not just the overseas student fees.'

Have a graduate student from overseas be available to newly arrived students from their particular country.

Educating the hosts or nationals on the need for being hospitable and friendly.

Staff and students should gradually establish a relationship.

The emphasis seems to be that the institution should not just value the overseas students for the high revenue their fees bring, but that the students' welfare should be the responsibility of the institution as well. UKCOSA (1986:20) argues that:

......if we accept that education may be treated as a market place commodity like any other, with market forces predominating, then surely we must be ready to face the challenges and responsibilities which this approach brings with it

According to The British Council (1989) considerable expense is involved by overseas students in studying in the UK; therefore, it is both morally right and sound business practice to provide value for money. Thus it should be a two-way relationship with the students providing needed resources and the university providing adequate support and satisfaction.

INDIVIDUAL AND GROUP INTERVIEWS

Individual and group interviews were conducted in 1996 to clarify issues raised in the questionnaires and to explore further the experience of specific groups like A. Postgraduate students, B. Theological students and C. Turkish students. D. Overseas Staff - there were further three interviews of overseas persons who did their research studies in different universities in the UK and are now employed as HE staff. The summary of the issues raised are presented below:

The individual and group interview questions were:
(i) What adjustment problems have you experienced?
(ii) What are your Coping Strategies?
(iii) What are your expectations of research supervision?
(iv) What suggestions would you make on what you consider helpful in the encounter between overseas students and staff.

CHAPTER EIGHT
INTERNATIONAL POST-GRADUATE STUDENTS' EXPERIENCE

Interviews of individual *Postgraduate* Students.

8.1. Profile of students interviewed

Four individual interviews were conducted among overseas postgraduate students in two different universities. One interview was tape-recorded. Those interviewed, one male and three female, were two Asians, one African and one Middle Eastern overseas student. Two were PhD students in Counselling and Agriculture in their second year of study and two were Masters Degree students in Tourism. in the final stages of their one year intensive programme.

8.2. Adjustment Problems
Academic

These students expressed problems they experienced because they did not have full departmental and institutional induction. They also said that differences in arrival time was not taken into account and the two who said they arrived after the institutions' opening date had no separate departmental induction.

The postgraduate students complained of no clear definition of the role of the supervisors. They said they were required to have a particular protocol in seeing the supervisor and sometimes they were not easily accessible. One said her method of communicating with her supervisors was through the 'pigeon holes' as she left messages for them in their letter box while they left their replies in her pigeon hole.

They complained of delays in returning draft chapters (some reported cases of up to three months' delay). There was also the concern of not being assisted to know that the research is their own and some say they have been stirred towards working on what their supervisors are familiar with rather than what they were sponsored to work on. The male Agriculture student said because there was no supervisor in the particular branch of agriculture he was sponsored to study, the supervisor to whom he was assigned tried to compel him to work in the supervisor's area of interest and eventually succeeded.

This male student referred to what he called 'Exploitation,' which he described as cases where students have been sent home at the end of the research-funding period without a degree but asked to continue with a project in their home countries. He said this had happened to three of his colleagues and because of the fear that it might happen to him he agreed to work in the area of his supervisor's interest rather than his sponsor's specification. When the researcher asked how he was going to explain this to his sponsors he said he was reading up his research area on his own while writing his thesis on the supervisor's area of interest because he did not wish his sponsorship time to run out.

One of the female students referred to a colleague who had two supervisors and each saw her at different times. They gave her conflicting instructions which affected her progress. She however said her own experience was different as her supervisors had joint meetings with her.

8.3. Personal and language problems
They all said they experienced homesickness. One of the female students said she had felt very insecure and inferior because of language difficulty. She said she had felt 'left out and an outsider' especially among home

students in her department. She said she had found this particularly disturbing because back in her home country she was a very confident and secure person. She said it took her a long time to adjust but that she had since regained her confidence.

A female student raised the issue of misunderstanding due to language difficulties and the need for supervisors to be specific and students to ask for clarification. She said that when she came back from her field trip her supervisor had said she should send in a chapter (without specifying which chapter). She had assumed it was a write-up of her field trip (but her supervisor meant the first chapter of the thesis). When she sent in what she thought was required her supervisor was not pleased with her, and according to her, it caused some misunderstanding which could have been avoided if the supervisor had been specific or if she had asked for clarification on what exactly the supervisor was expecting from her.

8.4. Social

All complained of apparent lack of interest in non-academic welfare of students. Their supervisors did not ask how they were settling in and adjusting to the new cultural and social systems. They also complained of apparent lack of trust and goodwill towards them as overseas students.

Some referred to the issue of 'role conflict' and 'status shock' They say that they and most of their postgraduate colleagues are mature students and had worked in their countries as lecturers and administrators and so required help to make the transition to student life. They said such help was not available and some said they had problems with such seemingly trivial things as the level of noise in the halls and the drink culture of some undergraduates.

8.5. Cultural differences

One female student highlighted the effect of cultural difference in the experience of a colleague. She said a postgraduate overseas student had to suffer in silence and this nearly cost her dearly because according to her, 'in Asian culture you do not contradict your seniors or embarrass them in public'. The said student was asked by her supervisors to reduce the content of her material for upgrade from MPhil to PhD document. At the internal viva her examiner noted that she knew more than her document gave her credit for and wondered why the document was scanty. Because she felt it was not right according to her culture to say that her supervisors had asked her to omit those details she said nothing. She was equally surprised that the supervisors made no attempt to point this out themselves. She was given time by the sympathetic examiner to include the omitted information in her work.

One of the female postgraduate students narrated an incident of 'transference' between her supervisor and herself. She said she noticed a negative reaction from her supervisor because he had negative information from elsewhere about her ethnic origin. She said she took time to correct the wrong information and immediately noticed a positive change of attitude on the part of her supervisor. This also highlights the need to avoid stereotypes of overseas students and the need to clarify any racial and cultural issues that may arise in cross-cultural contact.

8.6. Departmental issues

Those interviewed complained of lack of information and lack of adequate workplace facilities at departmental level. They stressed the lack of access and/or assistance in the use of sophisticated equipment or unfamiliar equipment These overseas postgraduate students asserted strongly that lack of familiarity with equipment on the part of the overseas student is not an indication of lack of ability.

Some said they needed some help at the initial stages in the use of such equipment as computers, copiers and fax machines. They noted that it was not all overseas students who had problems in this area but any who did were not assisted or given adequate information as to where to receive assistance e.g. the availability of computer classes.

At institutional level they all said they had a strong indication of 'not getting value for money' considering the income their fees generated.

8.7. Coping Strategies

A reoccurring coping strategy for those interviewed was making regular contacts with family at home. This they said was expensive but helpful in coping with homesickness and an encouragement to keep at their work and complete it successfully.

A female postgraduate student said how she felt like 'running back home' after her first three days abroad for the very first time. She said she phoned home and her mother encouraged her to persevere, which she had done. Her major coping strategy was to make long distance phone calls but this she found quite expensive.

The coping strategy of one postgraduate female student was to be outgoing. She took the initiative of mixing and making friends with overseas as well as with home students in her department. She also said that prayers and her faith in God were sources of help to her.

8.8. Expectations of Supervision

When they were individually asked what their expectations were of an outstanding supervisor, the following were their responses:

All of those interviewed said they expected their supervisors to be knowledgeable and, if possible, an expert in the area of the student's research. They also expected supervisors to be genuinely interested in the research student as a person and be able to respect and accept his/her cultural differences. Such a supervisor avoids stereotypes and generalisations that lead to misinterpretations and misunderstandings

Their expectations were that a supervisor would be concerned about the welfare of the student, e.g. whether they have adequate accommodation and also about their family welfare etc. They said they did not expect that the supervisor would be personally involved but should provide adequate information and refer students to appropriate support services.

They expected a supervisor to help students to accept the ownership of their research. And to encourage students to keep to promised time schedule which includes returning students' draft chapters within an acceptable time with written comments. Such a supervisor should act as a 'midwife' by piloting the student to a successful conclusion of the research study.

8.9. Suggestions

The suggestions of the postgraduate students interviewed were that there was need for cultural understanding between students and staff and that it would be beneficial for institutions to run courses for lecturers on cross-cultural issues.

A female student suggested that overseas student should take initiative in being friendly because in her experience some students respond to such contact.

They all recommended that for universities to attract more overseas students they should provide value for money.

CHAPTER NINE
INTERVIEWS WITH SPECIFIC GROUPS

GROUP INTERVIEW WITH THEOLOGICAL STUDENTS

9.1. A group interview was conducted with theological students who had previously completed the questionnaire. This was a mixed group of ten male and female overseas students from Africa, Asia and Latin America. The interview lasted for 60 minutes, was semi-structured and tape-recorded.

The students reiterated their responses given earlier in the survey and also added a few more points which are given below:

9.2 Adjustment Problems
Students felt that the one-week orientation they received was not enough.
Expectations and reality
A female student from Latin America felt that she had high expectations which were not met. She underestimated how long it would take her to gain a mastery of English language. Her estimation was six months but it actually took her two years. She also underestimated the effect of culture shock. She said everybody talked about it so much that she felt it would not be so bad but in reality it was a serious handicap for her. She said she did not find the British as outgoing and friendly as Latin Americans.

A male student from Ghana said he had realistic expectations because he had had contact with English expatriates in his own country who had made him aware of what to expect (This shows that pre-arrival preparation can benefit overseas students).

Most of the students said they expected to be able to get some part-time, preferably on-campus job to help them maintain a healthy financial status.

9.3. Personal

Some students from Asia and Africa said that they had difficulties of unrealistic expectations from home. Most received letters from relatives, who thought they were earning, asking them to buy them items they could not afford. One talked of 'letters with long shopping lists'.

9.4. Academic

All the participants said they found the transition from one academic system to another a challenge. They experienced language difficulty not in understanding members of staff but in getting people in general to understand them.

9.5. Cultural

They have all had to make very big adjustment on the issue of 'Time'. They found the British very time-conscious. They said that in their home countries people were less rigid with time and made allowances for others, even when it was not very convenient for them.

9.6. Social

The majority said they had formed no deep relationships which they said 'hurts'. They reported that people they had met more than once saw them on the street and went by without showing any signs that they had met before.

Elaborating on the unfriendly attitude of their hosts, an Indian student said he and his family had taken initiatives on several occasions to invite people for meals. The invitations were well received but these attempts led to no real friendship or lasting relationships.

9.7. Accommodation
Vacation accommodation was a major problem for most as they were expected to vacate their hostels during the vacation.

9.8. Religious
As these were theological students they were very keen to discuss the religious aspect of their experience. The majority said they came with the impression that Britain was a 'Christian country' but will be returning home with the conclusion that it is a 'secular country'. They said they have noted how, according to them, 'Christians are not able to influence the society in a positive way'.

9.9. Coping Strategies and suggestions for future students
When asked what their coping strategies were, the following were their responses:
- Maintain a goal - aim to accomplish the purpose for which you came.
- Be willing to adjust, e.g. to use first names where applicable.
- Take initiative to make friends, especially among other overseas students.
- Think international - Learn to relate to people of other cultures.

(iii) Good practice

When asked about the practices in their institution which they have found useful in their academic and personal adjustment. The following were their responses:

* The institution assigns ten students to one member of staff who looks after their academic and personal welfare. (It must be said that the population of this institution is small when compared with the population of most universities.)
* The Pastoral-care tutor had lived abroad for many years and this had a positive influence over her work. They all found her very understanding.
* The institution runs a re-entry workshop for students returning home to prepare them for reverse culture shock. The aim is to discuss changes and expectations that students will experience on getting back home.
* The institution promotes internationalism as three-quarters of the students are from overseas.

9.10. Students' suggestions for institutions

* One- to- one orientation would be more helpful. Continuing students to assist new students and, if possible, students from their own regions e.g. Asian students to assist other Asian students.
* Make provision for part-time jobs for students who need them.
* Change of attitude about stereotyped concepts of overseas students as people who must always be on the receiving end because of colonial history.
* Hosts to be more hospitable.

CHAPTER TEN
GROUP INTERVIEWS OF TURKISH MUSLIM STUDENTS

10.1. Four Turkish Muslim male students participated. These students had completed the questionnaires and agreed to be interviewed. Two interviews lasting 60 minutes each were conducted on two separate days. The interview was semi-structured and the questions were centred on the students' academic, social and personal experiences. They were asked how their experience matched their expectations, level and sources of assistance, coping methods, use of counselling facilities, etc. The students' names will be represented by their initials at their request.

The interview started with an informal discussion of reasons for coming to the UK to study. Students T and F came to the UK because they got scholarships to study here. Student A had a friend studying in the UK and student AL came here because the formalities were less than that of going to the USA. Moreover the duration of the MSc programme is one year which they all thought was a favourable option.

10.2. Expectations
F had higher expectations than reality. He found that facilities were inadequate, e.g. the accommodation was nothing like the impression he got from the brochures. For T. Expectation matched reality because he had previously studied in another foreign country (Germany).

Language was a bigger problem for F than he expected. T had studied abroad, so for him language was not a major problem. A.'s main expectation was academic which he said was fulfilled. His social expectation was confirmed in a negative way because he said he had heard that British people were generally not friendly and he found this to be so.

A had fewer expectations because he had travelled to many European countries.

10.3. Adjustment Problems

Language and academic

Their major problem was language difficulty which they said affected the possibilities of marketing their knowledge. They were particularly concerned with the problem of expression. When asked how much they took advantage of the language classes run for overseas students, their response was that there was little motivation to attend because it was the same level for all and that there was a care-free attitude of staff which was apparent. These students' observation was that many overseas students joined at the onset but there were very few at the end.

They said they thought that some lecturers had prejudices. They talked of subjective marking and said that having foreign name did not work in their favour.

They felt that they did not receive adequate feedback. For them 70% grade is not good enough. Nobody explains what happened to the other 30% of the mark! They said that, in some academic systems with which they were familiar it was possible to get 100% in some subjects. They said that comments on marks received and feedback on assignment would be helpful but that these were lacking.

10.4. Social

Other problems mentioned were racial discrimination e.g. F thinks British people do not like foreigners. All four reported having difficulty with local food. They felt that the institution did not make adequate provision to meet their needs. They gave examples of their specific needs as Muslims e.g. special toilet and shower facilities and dietary needs.

10.5. Assistance received

This they said depended on the nature of the problem.

They were grateful for the outside trips to places of interest organised by the Christian Union and International Students Christian Friends (ISCF - a Christian voluntary organisations on campus). However, they said that as Muslims, they would have been happier if these trips had been organised by the Student Union backed by financial assistance from the University administration.

10.6. Coping Strategies

They said they had no fixed strategy, but coped with issues as they arose. When asked if they had seen a counsellor before they said they have had no need for one.

10.7. Cultural Barriers

The students said they came from a 'close' culture where people are helpful but have not found this in the host culture which they described as 'distant'.

They said 'people are cold as the weather'.

They said there is respect for age in their home country which they do not see in the UK.

They noted some discrimination even among foreign students which the welfare staff were not aware of. Of greatest concern to them was the political strife between the Greek Cypriots and the Turkish Cypriots which was explosive even on campus. According to them nobody took it seriously when they reported.

10.8. Suggestions to Institutions

The following are the suggestions of these Turkish students to institutions:

- Provide adequate information.
- Have a complaint bureau.
- Employ an overseas person in the team work in the international office.
- Support Student Union International work with financial help.
- Make language classes meet the varied needs of overseas students.
- Improve facilities for overseas students.

CHAPTER ELEVEN

Individual Interviews of three overseas staff (of non-UK origin) who 'recently' completed their PhD and were employed in Universities in the UK

11.1. The interviews lasting 60 minutes each, were-tape recorded and followed a similar format. The interviewees were each asked to look back a few years and describe their experience as postgraduate students, the type of supervision they received, and the difficulties they encountered. They were asked about the coping strategies they used and finally to make recommendations to current and future postgraduate students. As two out of the three were currently personal tutors and supervisors, they were asked to suggest ways to enhance effectiveness in supervising overseas students. They were also asked to make recommendations to universities to enable them improve their provision for overseas students and thus maintain a steady or even an improved influx of overseas students.

The participants studied for their PhD in Universities in different parts of the UK. Their disciplines are Engineering and Language. They had been in University service for 1, 3 and 5years.

First Interview
11.2. Profile of Interviewee

This participant had a difficult first year as a postgraduate student, but in the end he did so well that he was employed by his University on completion of his studies. His initial relationship with his supervisors was not very good but by the third year it had so improved that he made several joint presentations at conferences with one of them.

11.3. Research experience

He was asked in the interview to describe his research experience. He said he had an initial meeting with the head of research in his department who mentioned names of persons to approach in different situations. However in terms of technical assistance he said he had little help.

When he was asked if he had structured or unstructured supervision he could not say which exactly it was. He said he had two supervisors who were not very involved with his research. One was very busy and the other was aloof. The busy one was interested in his work but gave him no attention.

At the onset he had written a general research plan and knew what his topic was. His expectation was that at his first meeting with his supervisors they would give him specific guidance at which point to start and from which area to start. He felt he was not given adequate induction. He was not told what facilities were available and what was not available. He stumbled into most things by chance. He said this initial stage was very stressful because of lack of direction.

He said it was a painful experience to spend time doing tasks to accomplish results that were already available without his knowing that they were available. Solutions to these tasks were there somewhere (e.g. in computer soft-ware) and he only needed someone to say they were there and show him how to locate them. Because he was not introduced to relevant soft-ware, he spent unnecessary time writing programmes instead of using existing ones to solve problems.

The consequence was that during his transfer exams from MPhil to PhD he found that he worked on his own with little or no input from his supervisors. The result was that he was told he had not taken proper account of what was expected of him.

This he said shocked him into reality and, as a mature student, he decided to take matters into his own hand and assume full responsibility for the research. He said that when he realised that his sponsorship time was running out he started asking for meetings to point out his frustrations, lack of progress, and to request access to certain facilities he was not given.

11.4. Relationship with his supervisors

The interviewee said his initial relationship with his supervisors were characterised (in his estimation) by serious lack of trust in his ability. Some of the facilities to which he was denied access were because of staffs' concern that he would ruin them.

He felt his supervisor's attitude was that he could not perform but that this attitude gradually changed after he took matters into his own hands and towards the end when they saw his worth.

His expectation was for more involvement from his supervisors, but said he only got occasional verbal interaction, and never had his supervisor by his side on the computer or in the laboratory looking at his work.

He emphasised that he did not expect his supervisors to solve his problems for him but he expected much more technical involvement. He expected help, to be pointed in the right direction, and expected to hear how the supervisors tacked such technical problems in their own student days. According to him they acted like people who were new in the area of study.

11.5. Relationship with colleagues

According to this interviewee it was either no relationship or a patronising relationship. In his estimation, it takes a long time for a personal friendly relationship to develop, time which he said overseas students do not have within the research period of three years or so.

He reported prejudice because of a media image of hunger and war. He said that poverty mentality was built into the image of UK students which often leads to a negative attitude towards overseas students. This makes it difficult for relationship to be on equal basis.

11.6. Coping Strategies

He said his coping strategy was to map out his own way. He narrowed down his research focus and moved from what he was advised to do to another area. He became more aware of what was available and decided to start publishing.

According to him an inspiration to succeed came with the feeling that he was not expected to succeed. He had to prove that wrong.

He got help from other overseas students. He was inspired by experience of two overseas MSc students who had performed so outstandingly well that one of them was awarded a scholarship to carry out a PhD research at Cambridge University.

He also said that as a committed Christian, his faith and trust in God saw him through. He had his family - wife and children - here which also helped.

11.7. Suggestions to current and future postgraduate students.

Based on his experience he made the following suggestions which are reproduced below:

Do not be overwhelmed by lack of familiarity with the computer or other facilities. Get information as fast as you can from those you can approach.

Be determined to succeed but do not be arrogant.
Get help from fellow overseas students, learn fast from them or other students and go on to do it yourself.

Do not feel inferior. Do not be an object of charity, do not accept other people's leftovers. Get it from the source e.g. do not accept out-dated soft-ware; you are entitled to new ones.

Be independent - financially and academically.

Take clues from other students as to how to address lecturers, supervisors and other members of staff etc. e.g. the use of first name.

11.8. Suggestions to supervisors

Believe the student is capable or else do not accept him or her in the first place.

Give information e.g. publications and direct them to departmental facilities, laboratories, library etc.

Be involved and monitor progress and give advice if the student is too slow.

Supervisors should not generally assume that lack of experience or exposure is the same as lack of ability on the part of the student. Some students from developing countries may have inadequate exposure to the use of such facilities as the computer but this should not be seen as lack of ability. Information will give the exposure.

Maintain some measure of trust. If students are denied access to facilities through lack of confidence in their ability to use them, that will cause a lot of setback.

It is a disadvantage to treat overseas students as if they know what is available. It is a double handicap to treat them as if they are dangerous to the facilities. In-depth departmental induction will ensure that they know what is available and are helped to use them.

11.9. Suggestions to Universities

The following were the interviewee's suggestions to universities to improve the adjustment process of overseas students.

Universities should have a member of staff from overseas to discuss with students from abroad. This individual can clarify things, e.g. duties, rights, and give information.

Universities should not be eager to recruit anyone for financial gain. It is a shame for anyone to spend £30,000 or more and not succeed. When students go back with bitterness and bad impression because of the way they were treated, they do nothing to advertise the university to others at home.

To promote the international image, students with language difficulties should be able to come and spend some time at language school at minimal cost.

The university should assist students to navigate their ways through the research experience by providing adequate induction programmes, helping them to work to full capacity and monitoring their progress.

Second Interview
11.2.1 Profile of interviewee
This participant had been a university staff member for three years. He had gained employment in a different university from where he studied. He drew from his experience and that of his research colleagues, and made recommendations based on his research experience and his current involvement in tutoring students from overseas.

11.2.2. Research experience
He said that he was unhappy with universities' recruitment policy. As a result of less money coming from central government he felt that recruitment drives were done with little grace. For instance, he said that, on getting to his university, he found that they had no specialist in his area. He was not alone in this as two of his colleagues, an Algerian and a Tunisian, had had similar problems. They had been admitted to do their research in translation work related to the Koran but there were no specialists in that area in their institution. The students ended up making private arrangements for an outside supervisor and had to pay for these themselves. He recalled that one of these students suffered from a high level of anxiety which affected that postgraduate student's work. He pointed out that there was some degree of negligence and academic dishonesty involved; he felt that it was not fair in view of the high fees overseas students pay.

11.2.3. Relationship with supervisor
According to him, he had very little feedback from his supervisor on the actual content of his work because it was not his supervisor's area of speciality. He recalled that his supervisor's regular comments were 'very

interesting'. He expected his supervisor to be a sounding board but that was not the case.

Coping strategies
He said he sought help elsewhere.

11.2.4 Problems overseas students face
The Interviewee was asked his views on problems overseas students' experience based on his current position as a personal tutor. The following were his responses:

11.2.5. Language difficulty.
His observation was that for most overseas students English is a second or third language and the degrees of problems of non-native speakers often vary. Framing of text, he said, was a common problem. In his experience some Greek students have a lot of structural problems. This he said could affect the assessor who may need to rate content above style. He also noted that some Indian students were 'flowery' in their style of presentation which made them lose marks.

11.2.6. Different educational system.
He pointed out that most overseas students come from different educational systems that have different expectations. Different systems have different methods of assessment which create expectations in the learners as to what the assessors want in order to get a pass grade. When the student switches systems he/she has not become worse it is only that the system is different. His observation was that it results in an ego-

damaging experience for some overseas students when this is not handled with care.

He recalled the case of three Japanese students, in his department, who withdrew because of loss of face when they got average marks in their first assignment. In their background average mark would have been a poor mark.

11.2.7 Suggestions to current and future postgraduate students

In the light of his experience and observations he recommended that overseas students should:

Find an understanding person to relate to who can make you comfortable about your competence and assure you that you are as good as you were but the system is different and that you need to adjust to the new system. This will rebuild your confidence and motivate you to progress.

Adapt to the new educational system.

11.2.8. Suggestions to staff working with overseas students

Increase your tolerance level when working with students who are non-native English speakers.

Give detailed feedback on assignments as this will assist students.

Be aware that most have come from different academic systems with different expectations.

Make students feel at home, no matter what their background is, prejudice or bias when shown blocks learning.
Be sensitive to the needs of the learners.

Avail yourself of seminars on cross-cultural issues where these are available.

11.2.9. Recommendations to Universities

Ensure that your recruitment policy is honest. Students should not be recruited when the University has no expert in their area.

Students expect a fair deal considering the high fees they pay.

Third Interview
11.3.1. Profile of interviewee
The third interviewee had been in university service for over five years. He had a good relationship with his supervisor as a postgraduate student. He had not experienced much difficulty with the system because he had studied in another western country for his first degree. His recommendations were based mainly on his current role as a lecturer and supervisor of home and overseas students.

11.3.2. Research Experience
In his experience universities admitted students and assigned them to the lecturer nearest to their research area. This means that most of the time the supervisors were not necessarily experts in the students' area of interest. Sometimes the supervisors convinced students to do what interests them rather than the students. He had observed cases where students had started on the topic proposed by their supervisors and had

discovered after about a year that they were not making much progress in that area and the project was abandoned for something else, resulting in waste of time and resources. He said that the solution is for research students to be fairly sure of what they want to work on.

He also observed that many overseas students tended to do fundamental research which fits into a time schedule, while most home students often did sponsored projects which are obtained from research institutions and therefore structured.

He also pointed out that overseas students often experienced accommodation problems because most were mature married students who had children. Most universities did not have adequate or enough married couples' accommodation for students. He noted that worrying over accommodation could be very distracting for research students.

11.3.3. Relationship with supervisor

He said he *had a good relationship* with his own supervisor. This he said was marked by mutual respect. At the start of the research he said his supervisor convinced him to take on a research contract of the supervisor's choice but when this fizzled out he was supported in his own choice of topic.

11.3.4. Suggestions to current and future postgraduate students

He made extensive suggestions to current and future postgraduate students based on his experience as a former overseas postgraduate student and from his current post as lecturer, personal tutor and supervisor. The suggestions are reproduced below:

Know the area of your research and the purpose of the research. Structure what you want to do in stages.

Be aware that research is an independent study. The degree is yours and the lecturer is there to help.

It is best to choose a research area that has been researched before and fit in what you want to do with that as a background.

Time and sponsorship are not limitless.

Find out about the university system and understand how to use facilities like the library etc.

Sort out family and financial issues at the beginning to avoid unnecessary stress. Secure adequate accommodation for your family to avoid distractions. This is one of the important things to look for before accepting an offer of admission.

Avail yourself of language lessons if you have language difficulty.

There is no hard and fast rule as every project is different but the lecturer is there to assist and direct the student to achieve his objective. Get as much help as you can on how to draw up your questions and make the necessary contacts.

By the end of the first year you should assume control of your work and have the transfer exams scheduled for the end of the year.

Transfer exams give the opportunity to say what you are doing. You do not need to have known everything or done everything. You need to convince the examiner why you need to research the area and that you understand what you need to do and also to show how much you have already done and what is left to be done. You need to show that you have enough time and funding to complete the research.

Avoid a situation where the funding or time runs out and the project comes to an abrupt end.

Your research should be unique. Pick out what others have done, acknowledge them, understand them and report them in your own words and make it flow in your stream of thought.

Good relationship with your supervisors is essential.

11.3.5. Suggestions to supervisors

Be aware and sensitive to the needs of overseas students and assist them the best you can.

Ensure that a good relationship exists between you and your research students.

11.3.6. Suggestions to Universities

Have a good accommodation policy especially for postgraduate overseas students who are mostly married and have children. This is what most students look for before accepting an offer of admission. This prevents family accommodation concerns which distract students.

Have a good recruitment policy. Do not recruit students with serious language difficulty who will withdraw only after the first year. Ensure adequate provision for students.

CHAPTER TWELVE
CONCLUSION AND RECOMMENDATIONS

CONCLUSION

12.1. This study has investigated the experience of international/overseas students in UK higher education as well as factors that create barriers in counselling and working with them. There were similarities between the problems of overseas students as they reported themselves and their problems as viewed by staff and counsellors *(These will be clearer by the views of Counsellors and the views of Academic and Non- academic staff that will follow in the next two publications)*. Moreover there were similarities in what the three groups saw as barriers in counselling and working with overseas students arising from differences in academic systems and expectations, cultural differences and language difficulties. The three groups suggested that there should be increased awareness of overseas students' adjustment problems and the issues that create barriers; that overseas students should be given cultural orientation to help them to adapt to UK academic, cultural and social systems; that institutions should provide and encourage all staff to attend cultural awareness training/workshops; that institutions should ensure that an overseas person (with whom students can identify) is a member of the support services team; that institutions should be seen to be providing overseas students with value for money and to demonstrate how good support for overseas students while they are here in the UK will lead to goodwill towards the institution and the UK when they return home. Based on this study recommendations have been made to staff, counsellors and institutions as to what will improve the experience of overseas students and factors that will enhance effectiveness in counselling and working with overseas students. Recommendations were also made to the Students Union to raise awareness of overseas students' experience and encourage home students to extend some hospitality to their overseas colleagues and ensure some integration. Finally some recommendations have been made to future and current overseas students encouraging them to adapt to the UK systems while maintaining their cultural identity. Coping strategies were also recommended with the view that overseas students should make the most of their study in UK higher education.

RECOMENDATIONS

12.2. In the three main sections of the study, students, staff, and counsellors have made suggestions to students, to staff and to institutions. Based on these what now follows is a comprehensive recommendation from the study. These are practical and theoretical implications of the research which are presented as recommendations for different groups. The recommendations are to Staff (academic and non-academic) especially to personal tutors and supervisors, Counsellors, Heads of Departments and Senior Institutional Managers, The Students Union and Overseas Students.

The author recognises that as a second language user the recommendations may sound too direct. The recommendations are not meant to be prescriptive, but based on the research findings, the author hopes that they will be a source of information for those who are interested in the experiences of international/overseas students and staff (academic and non- academic) who work with them.

As said earlier, this study does not lay claim on generalisation of the findings but on extrapolation. **This means that the findings of this study are intended to enhance the <u>understanding</u> of the experience of international/overseas students** (from Asia, Africa, Latin America and the Middle East) in UK higher education **and the experience of some counsellors and staff working with them.**

These recommendations are also made in the understanding that:

Overseas students are good for our (UK) universities and other centres of higher learning to the point of being essential. They are certainly good for British students. They are good for Britain economically and for her relations with other countries. Their coming to study in Britain is good for overseas students themselves, as long as they are properly provided for, and good for the countries they come from.

(Overseas Students' Trust (OST) 1987:x)

12.3. Recommendations for staff

Some suggestions follow to enhance effectiveness for members of staff who work with overseas students. Some suggestions are intended for all such staff while some are specific recommendations for personal tutors and supervisors.

Improving the experience of overseas students - Recommendations for staff
<u>Increasing cultural awareness</u>
It is recommended that staff would benefit from increasing their cross-cultural knowledge, awareness and skills through reading, contact with people of other cultures and participation in cross-cultural awareness workshops. That staff be sensitive to the needs of overseas students and be aware that most have come from different academic systems with different expectations. That staff be sensitive to how language difficulties and cultural differences can lead to misinterpretations and misunderstanding between staff and overseas students.

Examining assumptions and stereotypes

It is recommended that staff should examine their implicit assumptions and stereotypes about overseas students; to make them explicit when they can; and then to question their validity. That staff should initiate exploration with overseas students to clarify the meanings behind any verbal or non-verbal communication which makes them feel uncomfortable, e.g. avoidance of eye contact, hand-shake, smiles and bows, interpersonal space and use of first names. That staff should show an interest in the welfare of their overseas students, by finding out about appropriate support services so that they can make referral should it be necessary.

12.4. Some suggestions are directed to personal tutors and supervisors

Roles and expectations

It is recommended that at the onset of research or study programme, specific attention could be devoted to negotiating the respective roles of supervisor and student or tutor and tutee, and their mutual expectations of one another. To explain research and study approaches in the UK system (which is often different from systems overseas students are used to back home) and any professional etiquette they need to know.

Supervisors are to assist students to accept responsibility for their research. Those supervisors should monitor the progress of their students who should give them regular written feedback. Supervisors will do well to assist overseas research students to work within their time schedules and to keep to their research deadlines.

It is recommended that supervisors should assume the role of a 'midwife' by piloting the students to a successful conclusion of the research study. Supervisors to act before potential problems escalate and get out of hand

and where appropriate lobby management to improve the provision for overseas research students who work throughout the year.

It would be helpful for Staff to increase their tolerance level when working with students who are non-native English speakers. If possible, to speak slowly and avoid idioms and slang. Staff to ensure the use of overhead projector and handouts in lectures. Supervisors to give freedom for research students to approach other lectures for help, if area is outside supervisor's expertise according to National Postgraduate Committee recommendation (NPC, 1995:5).

12.5. Recommendations for Heads of Departments and Institutional Management.

As each institution has its own norms about what responsibilities are delegated from central control down to departments, so some of the following recommendations are for heads of department, for their nominees as departmental postgraduate tutors or an equivalent, and some are for institutional managers. Responsibilities which are most likely to be departmental are at the beginning and those most likely to be the institutional are at the end.

Recommendations For Heads of Department and Institutional Managers.

Some recommendations are directed to Heads of Department

From the study it is recommended that departmental heads should provide cultural orientation for overseas students on arrival and that such departmental and institutional induction should include access to facilities.

That some form of repeat induction be included in welcome programmes to accommodate research students who arrive at non-standard points in the academic year. That it is necessary to provide a protected and adequate workspace for research students and that departmental facilities be made available during vacations as these students work all the year round.

Institutional Managers

The study recommends that institutions' managers should provide realistic pre-admission information, including specific information on availability and nature of accommodation, and on such facilities as support services. They should take language requirements seriously in recruitment to avoid wastage through drop-out for those with serious language difficulties.

Managers should provide detailed information about the host department and the academic interests of potential supervisors. **They should ensure that research students are admitted only when the institution has supervisors whose areas of expertise include the focus of the overseas students' research project**. To ensure the provision of adequate accommodation for both undergraduate and postgraduate students, especially family accommodation with child-care facilities for married students, where possible.

Managers could recruit postgraduate students from overseas to assist in welcoming newly arrived students from their particular region, if possible. They should assign a member of academic or administrative staff with special responsibility for overseas students and if possible this intermediary staff should be seen to be an overseas person.

Managers should device ways to increase awareness among staff and students of the experiences and potential difficulties of overseas students e.g. through talks organised by the overseas /national student societies. They should organise cultural awareness workshops and training and <u>provide incentives to encourage staff to attend and increase their cross-cultural skills</u>. They should encourage, and where possible, provide modest funds, to operate overseas students/or national societies.

Managers should ensure the circulation of relevant codes of practice and regular updated publicity on services and facilities. They should provide a channel whereby overseas students can give feedback to supervisors/tutors, departments and institutions without fear of repercussions. They should organise interviews or some other means by which all parties can check that the student, the department and supervisor are suitably matched.

They should make adequate institutional facilities available during vacations, since research students, particularly overseas research students, work through vacations. They should ensure that there is a link between the international office and different services that work with overseas students. They should promote religious tolerance and ensure that staff and students do not criticise what others believe and be sensitive to such religious requirement of some students e.g. type of food and avoiding the serving of alcohol during official reception for overseas students.

They should ensure that departments and institutions are seen to be giving overseas students <u>value for money</u> . This satisfies the overseas students and pays dividends in the long run because a satisfied customer is the best possible marketing agent for acquiring new students.

12.6. Recommendations for Counsellors

Counsellors working with overseas students should be aware and sensitive to the needs of overseas students e.g. adjustment issue and language difficulties. They should increase their awareness and sensitivity and knowledge of other cultures through reading, training and workshops. They should develop an awareness of their own culture.

They should avoid generalisations and stereotypes and treat overseas students as individuals. It is recommended that they should 'learn' from the overseas student client about who would be competent and willing to help with the problem in their culture and how such help would be given.

Counsellors should be flexible in their counselling approach, using either a directive or a non-directive approach or a combination of both depending on the problem and the context. But be aware that the forms of counselling practised in the UK are European in origin and are not necessarily helpful to clients from other cultures who may be seeking guidance in counselling.

Counsellors are to modify clients' expectations of counselling. Also to modify counsellor's communicative style to accommodate clients for who English is a foreign or second language.

Counsellors should be explicit about cultural differences. And be aware of transference and counter-transference as well as issues of racial prejudice and discrimination. Counsellors should 'Bracket off' their assumptions and preconceived ideas and clarify any non-verbal communication issues with overseas student clients, e.g. eye contact and interpersonal space.

Counsellors should be aware of how language difficulties, cultural differences and religious beliefs can create barriers in counselling international/overseas students. *Also to be aware that, no matter how broad a counsellor's knowledge of other cultures is, the tendency is that he/she will be limited by his/her world view.*

12.7. Recommendations for Students Unions

Students Unions should raise awareness about the experiences of overseas students, especially the barriers created by cultural differences and language difficulties. They should encourage home students to be friendlier to overseas students. To ensure that activities for overseas students do not exclude UK students, so that there is more integration.

Student Union should provide information and assist in the induction programmes, where they can, especially at the departmental level. *To ensure that services for international/overseas students are more pro-active rather than reactive.*

They should organise cultural awareness seminars and workshop for student's union staff and extend it to all students. Encourage UK students who have been abroad to talk about their experiences as foreign students to groups in the Student Union and the University. *Where possible, lobby management to improve the provision for overseas students considering the high fees they pay.*

Be sensitive to religious beliefs of overseas students and the implications for their use of Students' Union facilities. Variety is often needed to cater for most overseas students' dietary tastes and religious requirements. They should assist overseas students by arranging for catering services to include dishes like rice and other varieties *and should provide information on where foreign food items can be purchased outside the institution.*

12.8. Recommendations for Overseas Students including Coping Strategies.

The following are recommendations for future and current overseas students and these include coping strategies.

<u>Before arrival</u> overseas students should ensure that they confirm accommodation provision. They should be sure that their institution has the course they hope to pursue and if they are postgraduate, *confirm that they will be assigned to a supervisor whose areas of expertise include their research interest.*

Overseas students should ensure that their English is adequate for studying in the UK or else make arrangements in their home country to attend language classes to improve their English-language competence. They should find out all they can about the effect of culture shock and how they can deal with it. They should read about the way of life and the people of the UK. *They should ensure that they have good financial arrangements, and be prepared for the cold weather.*

They should come with realistic expectations as there are both advantages and disadvantages in studying in a different culture.

<u>On arrival</u> overseas students should request for cultural orientation as part of their institution's welcome pack. They should be aware of the experience of culture shock and some adjustment problems because of the new environment.

Academic issues

Overseas students should be aware that there could be differences between the <u>academic system</u> they are used to and the British academic system. They should be willing and ready to adjust to the new system if they are going to be successful. Should be aware that the UK academic system involves <u>interactive learning</u>. Students may be expected to be active in class.

They should be aware that <u>making choices</u> is important in the UK system. Students often have a degree of personal choice in their selection of research, essay or project topics. To be aware that many members of staff, including supervisors and personal tutors, often expect to be addressed by their <u>first names</u>. Should take a cue from how other students address them. To be aware that there is <u>gender equality</u> in the UK institutions of higher learning, this means that female and male members of staff are equally respected and accepted.

Cultural issues

Overseas students should be sensitive to cultural differences as things may be done and seen differently from what and ways they are used to in their home country for example, they should be aware that the approach to <u>time</u>-keeping is very rigid in the UK for instance, to arrive late in often considered impolite or a disregard for the person one is meeting or the lecture/seminar one is attending. They should be aware that interpersonal <u>space</u> is maintained in the UK as people usually keep a certain distance, unlike in other cultures where people stand quite close to each other while in conversation.

Overseas students should be aware that in the UK people often do not <u>touch</u> others during a conversation as is the case in some other cultures where one may touch or hug people on as many occasions as possible. They should be aware that the meaning of non-verbal communication (<u>gestures</u> and body language) may vary from culture to culture. *It is better to clarify meaning from others than to assume that it means the same as in one's own country.*

They should be aware that in the UK most people smile as a way of greeting and people always maintain eye contact in conversation. Should be aware that this is different from some other cultures where people do not look older people or authority figure straight in the eye.

Social Issues

Overseas students should be aware that different societies give different interpretations to the giving of gifts. While in some cultures gifts are given at any time to show appreciation, in British culture gifts are sometimes only exchanged on occasions between friends. They should be sensitive to this so that their gifts are not regarded as a bribe.

They should be aware that the British are known to be reserved in nature and are very reluctant to show their emotions in public (except in football matches!). They might misinterpret any loud and obvious show of emotion in a conversation as being aggressive. The British are also known to be polite. They often make a request in an indirect way and may misunderstand direct demands as being rude and offensive.

They should be aware that most UK students (and people) often mind their own business, visitors (and foreigners) to the UK see them as unfriendly. They should be prepared to adapt to the ways of doing things in the UK institution and society while maintaining their cultural identity. *International students returning home after their studies should be aware of reverse culture shock and the need to learn to re-adjust to their own culture and society.*

Research Students

International/Overseas students should remember that the research is theirs; this means that they should know the area of their research and the purpose of the research. They should be aware that they should structure their work in stages and remember that their time and sponsorship are limited. Overseas research students should assume control of the research and prepare for the transfer examination by the end of the first year.

They should strive to maintain good relationships with their supervisors.

12.9. Coping strategies for Overseas Students.

Overseas students should be certain of their goal for coming to study in the UK and should work to achieve it and be willing to adjust to the new academic and social system. They should avail themselves of in-session language classes if they need them.

Overseas students should be aware that other students from their home country (especially those in their second or third year in the UK) could provide guidance and information as to where to buy familiar food items. They should join cultural and ethnic associations in their institution to keep them from feeling lonely and isolated and to maintain their cultural identity.

They should join clubs and sporting activities as these provide excellent opportunity to socialise and interact with British students, which can help to improve conversational English. Overseas students should not spend all their time studying, but should spare a few hours and take some initiatives to make friends among other overseas students, not just those from their country of origin.

Overseas students should be aware that some voluntary organisations working among overseas students in universities in the UK sometimes 'pair' British students (who are willing) with overseas students to provide informal cultural orientation. This is not an 'arranged friendship'. The British student may be able to assist an overseas student in specific areas, but may not necessarily be available at a social level. They should be aware of this from the start to avoid misunderstanding.

Overseas students should not be overwhelmed by lack of familiarity with the computer or other facilities, they should get as much information as they can and attend classes to learn to use them. They should secure adequate accommodation for themselves and their family, where applicable, so as to concentrate on their studies and as much as possible be financially independent.

BIBLIOGRAPHY

Ackers, J. Evaluating UK courses: The perspective of the Overseas Student. in McNamara, D. and Harris, R (Ed) 1997 **Overseas Students in Higher Education**, London: Routledge.

Adam, J. 1965 **Counselling and Guidance: A summary view.** London: Macmillan.

Allen, A & Higgins, T. 1994 **Higher Education: The International Student Experience**. Leeds: Heist Publication.

Alder, P. S. The Traditional Experience: An Alternative View of Culture Shock. **Journal of Humanistic Psychology** 15, 13-23, 1975.

Alexander, et al. 1976 Psychotherapy and the Foreign Student In Pedersen, P. et al.(ed.) **Counselling Across Cultures.** Hawaii: Honolulu University Press.

Al-Shawi, R. L 1990 Multi-Cultural Counselling: An Investigation of the Problems of Overseas Students In Britain and Their Perceived Need For Help. Unpublished PhD Thesis: Keel University.

Althen, G. (ed.)1994 **Learning Across Cultures.** Washington DC. NAFSA.

Althen, G. 1994. **The Handbook of Foreign Student Advising**. Yarmouth, ME: Intercultural Press.

Ames, M. 1996 Oxford Brookes: The International Student Experience. A report of a survey of decision-making motivations and experiences of non-EU students on undergraduate courses at Oxford Brookes University.

Animashawun, G. African Students in Britain. **RACE Journal**. 5, 38-47, 1963.

Anumonye, A. 1970. **African Students in Alien Cultures**. New York: Black Academy Press.

Augsburger, D.W. 1986 **Pastoral Counselling Across Cultures**. Philadelphia, USA: The Westminster Press.

Barker, J. The Purpose of Study, Attitude to Study and Staff-Student Relationships in McNamara, D. and Harris, R (Ed) (1997) **Overseas Students in Higher Education** London: Routledge.

Bochner, S 1972 **Overseas students in Australia.** New South Wales: University Press.

Bock, P (ed.) 1970 **'Culture Shock' a Reader in Modern Psychology**, New York: Knopf

British Association of Counselling, (BAC) 1 Regent Place, Rugby, Warwickshire.

Brown, G. 1988: Culture and culture Shock, **Helping Overseas Students to Succeed.** A practical Guide for those Working with Overseas Students. Nottingham: NACOSA.

Brown, G and Atkins, M 1988 **Effective Teaching in Higher Education.** London: Routledge.

British Council 1990 **Studying and Living in Britain.** UK: Northcote House Publishing.

British Council 1991 and 1997 **Feeling at Home** A Guide to Cultural Issues for those Involved in Housing Overseas Students.

Black, T. 1993: **Evaluating Social Science Research: An Introduction**, London: Sage Publications.

Bloor, M. and Bloor, T 1991 Cultural Expectation and Socio-pragmatic failure in academic writing', **Review of ELT** (special issue on socio-cultural issues in English for academic Purposes), 1-12.

Bryman, A. Quantity and Quality in Social Research in Martin Bulmer (ed.) 1988. **Contemporary Social Research services**. London Macmillan.

Bulmer, M. 1979 Concepts in the Analysis of Qualitative Data. **Sociological Review.** 27(4):651-79.

Campbell, D. and Stanley, J. 1963. Experimental and quasi-experimental designs for research on teaching, in N. Gage (ed.), **Handbook of Research on Teaching**. Chicago: Rand McNally.

Carlton, E. 1994 Tough but Tender Line Strikes a Chord in **Times Higher Education Supplement** (THES) 30/9/94 p vi.

Chan, D. and Drover, G. 1997 Teaching and Learning for Overseas Students: The Hong Kong Connection in McNamara, D. and Harris, R (Ed) 1997 **Overseas Students in Higher Education** London: Routledge.

Channell, J. The Student-Tutor Relationship in Kinnell (ed.) 1990 **The Learning Experiences of Overseas Students**. Buckingham: SRHE and Open University Press.

Cheng, L. L. Recognising Diversity. A need for a Paradigm Shift. **American Behavioural Scientist** 34, (2) 263-278, 1990.

Church, A.T. Sojourner Adjustment. **Psychology Bulletin** 91(3) 540-572, 1982.

Clegg, F. 1990 **Simple Statistics.** UK: Cambridge University Press.

Clifford, J. Adlerian Therapy in Dryden, W.(ed.) 1996 **Handbook of Individual Therapy.**, London: Sage Publication.

Cohen, L. & Manion, L. 1989. **Research Methods in Education**: 3rd edition. London: Routledge.

Corey, G. 1996. Overview of Contemporary Counselling Models and Contribution to Multicultural Counselling. **The Theory and Practice of Counselling and Psychotherapy.** London: Pacific Grove.

Committee of Vice Chancellors and Principals (CVCP) 1992b. **The Management of Higher Degrees Undertaken by Overseas Students** Code of Practice, N/95/177, London: CVCP.

CVCP 1995a **Economic Impact of International Students in UK Higher Education.** London: CVCP.

CVCP 1995b **Recruitment and Support of International Students in UK Higher Education**. London: CVCP.

Cortazzi, M and Jin, L. Communication for Learning Across Cultures in McNamara, D. and Harris, R (Ed) 1997 **Overseas Students in Higher Education.** London: Routledge.

Cox, C. 1988 Acculturative stress and world view. Unpublished doctoral dissertation. Ohio State University.

Christensen, C. P. A Perceptual Approach to Cross-Cultural Counselling **Canadian Counsellor** 19, 2, 63-81, 1985.

Cronbach, L.J. 1982. **Designing Evaluation of Educational and Social Programs**. San Francisco: Jossey-Brass.

Cryer, P. 1996. **The Research Student's Guide to Success**, Buckingham: Open University Press.

Cryer, P. and Okorocha, E. Supervisors from Western Tradition and Research Students from Non-English Speaking Backgrounds: Potential Pitfalls and their Avoidance' in Zuber-Skerritt, O. 1998 **Supervising Postgraduate Students from Non-English-Speaking Backgrounds**. (In press) Buckingham: Open University Press.

D'Ardenne, P and Mahtani, A 1989. **Transcultural Counselling in Action**. London: Sage Publication.

Dearing Report 1997 **Higher Education in the Learning Society.** Summary Report. London : NCIHE./ THES 25/7/1997.

Denzin, N.K. 1970. **The Research Act in Sociology.** London: Butterworths.

Denzin, N.K. 1993. **Strategies of Multiple Triangulation: Sociological Methods**: A Source Book. New York: McGraw-Hill.

Dey, I. 1993. **Qualitative Data Analysis.** London: Routledge.

Dillard, J.M. and Chisolm, G. Counselling the International Student In a Multicultural Context **Journal of College Student Personnel,** March 1983, 101-105.

Dodge, S. Culture Shock and Alienation Remain Problems For Many Foreign Students On U.S. Campuses. **The Chronicles of Higher Education,** March 7, 1990, A33-A35.

Dryden, Windy (ed.) 1996 **Handbook of Individual Therapy** London: Sage Publications.

Eide, I. (Ed) 1970 **Students as Links between Cultures.** Oslo: UNESCO.

Elsey, B. Teaching and Learning in Kinnell (ed.) 1990. **The Learning Experiences of Overseas Students**. Buckingham: SRHE and Open University Press.

Eleftheriadou, Z. 1994. **Transcultural Counselling**. London: Central Book Publishing.

Elton, L. Teaching and tutoring international students, in Shotnes (ed.) 1985. **The Teaching and Tutoring of International Students.** London: UKCOSA Workshop report.

Esen, A. A view of Guidance from Africa. **Personnel and Guidance Journal**, 50, 792-799, 1972.

Exum, A.H. and Lau, E.Y. Counselling Style Preference of Chinese College Students. **Journal of Multicultural Counselling and Development** 16, 85-92,1988.

Fouad, N Training Counsellors to Counsel International Students: Are We Ready? **The Counselling Psychologist**, 19(1) 66-71,1991.

Fernando, S. 1991. **Mental Health, Race and Culture.** London: Macmillan.

Fisher, S. et al 1985. Homesickness, Health and Efficacy in first year Students. Jornal of Environmental Psychology, 5, 181-95.

Furnham, A. The Experience of Being an Overseas Student in McNamara, D. and Harris, R (Ed) 1997 **Overseas Students in Higher Education.** London: Routledge.

Furnham, A and Bochner, S. 1986. **Culture Shock: Psychological reaction to unfamiliar environment**. London: Methuen.

Furnham, A and Bochner, S. 1982. Social Difficulty in a Foreign Culture: An empirical analysis of culture shock. In S. Bochner (ed.) **Cultures in Contact: Studies in Cross- Cultural Interaction**. Oxford: Pergamon.

Furnham , A. and Tresize. The mental health of foreign students **Social science and Medicine**, 17,365-70, 1983.

Goetz, J. P. and LeCompte, M. D. 1984. **Ethnography and Qualitative Design in Education Research**. Orlando, FL: Academic Press.

Goldsmith, J. and Shawcross, V. 1985. **It Ain't Half Sexist Mum: Women as Overseas Students in the UK.** London: Joint UKCOSA and World University Service Publication.

Guba, E.G. and Lincoln, Y.S. 1988. **Naturalistic Inquiry.** London: Sage Publications.

Hall, E. T. 1966. **The Hidden Dimension**. New York: Anchor Press/Doubleday.

Hall, E. T. 1959. **The Silent Language**. New York: Doubleday.

Hall, M. 1976. **Strangers in Birmingham.** Birmingham: BICSA Publication.

Harris, R. Overseas Students in the United Kingdom University System: A Perspective from Social work. in McNamara, D. and Harris, R (Ed) 1997 **Overseas Students in Higher Education.** London: Routledge.

Hammersley, M & Atkinson, P. 1992. **Ethnography: Principles In Practice.** London: Routledge.

Hammersley, M. (ed.) 1993. **Social Research: Philosophy, Politics and Practice.** London: Sage Publication.

Heikinheimo & Shutte: The Adaptation of Foreign Students: Students Views and Institutional Implications. **Journal of Counselling and Student Personnel,** Sept. 1986.

Hesselgrave, D. J. 1979 **Communicating Christ Cross-Culturally.** Michigan: Zondervan.

Hesselgrave, D. J. 1984. **Counselling-Cross-Culturally: An Introduction to Theory & Practice for Christians.** USA: Baker Book Company.

HESA Data Report 1995. Students in Higher Education Institutions.

Higginbotham, J.B. and Cox, K. K. 1979. **Focus Group Interviews.** Chicago: American Marketing Association.

Hofstede, G. 1980. **Cultural Consequences: International Differences in Work Related Values.** Beverley Hills: Sage Publications.

Howarth, A.. Overseas Students in the UK: The Government's Position (Conservative party perspective) **Journal of International Education** 2 (1), 9-18, 1991.

Hughes, S. and Read, K. From Subsidy to Scholarship: A Retrograde Step' (Liberal Democrat party perspective). **Journal of international Education,** 2 (1), 29-43, 1991.

Hunt, J. 1989. **Psychoanalytic Aspects of Fieldwork.** London: Sage Publications,

Idowu, A .I. Counselling Nigerian Students In United States Colleges and Universities. **Journal of Counselling and Development,** 63, 506-509, 1985.

Ivey, E 1988. **International Counselling and Interviewing.** Monterey, CA: Brooks/Cole.

Jarvis, P. 1994 Education and Qualification (Seminar Presentation) Dept of Educational Studies, University of Surrey. Guildford.

Jackson, M. 1996 Muticultural Counselling: Historical Perspectives' in Ponterotto, J. Casas, J. Suzuki, L. Alexander, C. (ed.) 1996 **Handbook of Multicultural Counselling.** London: Sage Publications.

Jenkins, R. A Student-Centred Induction Programme for International Students. **Journal of International Education.** 1(3) 59-63, 1990.

Johnson, D. C. Problems of Foreign Students. **International Educational and Cultural Exchange,** VI, 61-68, 1971.

Kareem, J. and Littlewood, R. 1992. **Intercultural Therapy: Themes, Interpretations and Practice.** Oxford: Blackwell Scientific Publications.

Kareem, J. The Nafsiyat Intercultural Therapy Centre: Ideas and Experience in Intercultural Therapy in Kareem. J. and Littlewood, R. 1992. **Intercultural Therapy: Themes, Interpretations and Practice.** Oxford: Blackwell Scientific Publications.

Kahne, M. Cultural Differences: Whose Troubles Are We Talking About ? **International Educational and Cultural Exchange,** XI(4) 36-40, 1976.

Kauffmann, N. 1992 **Students Abroad: Strangers at Home.** Education for a Global Society, Yarmouth, Maine: Intercultural Press.

Keenan, S. View From the Face: Survey of Overseas Students Currently Studying in the UK. **Education for Information** 10, (4) 299-305, 1992.

Keech, M. Supporting for development: the QUT experience, paper presented at the Australia Development Studies Network Symposium, Canberra, Sept. 23-24, 1994.

Kennedy, E. and Charles, C. 1990. **On Becoming a Counsellor** Dublin: Gill and Macmillan.

Kinnell, M The Marketing and Management of Courses in Kinnell (ed.) 1990. **The Learning Experiences of Overseas Students**. Buckingham: SRHE and Open University Press..

Klineberg, O. & Hull, W.F. 1979. **At a foreign University. An International Study of Adaptation and Coping**. New York: Praeger Publishers.

Klineberg, O. 1976 Counselling in International Perspective Opening address of the seventh Round Table in Wurzburg

Klopper, A. 1991 Furthering Internationalism: Provision for Overseas Students at the University of Surrey Guildford. Unpublished MSc Thesis.

Kohls, L and Knight, J. 1994 **Developing Intercultural Awareness** Yarmouth, Maine: Intercultural Press.

Koyama, T 1992. **Japan: A handbook in Intercultural Communication.** Sydney: Clarendon.

Lago, C.& Clark, J 1980 The Necessary Sensitivity: The History and Development of some Guidelines for those Engaged in Cross-cultural Counselling. Unpublished paper.

Lago, C. 1989: Status of Multicultural Counselling in Britain: Challenges of Cultural and Racial Diversity to Counselling, London Conference Proceedings, **American Association for Counselling and Development** (p1-3)

Lago, C.O. 1991. **Working With Overseas Students.** A Staff Development Training Manual, Huddersfield Polytechnic and British Council.

Lago, C.O. Some Complexities In Counselling International Students. **Journal of International Education.** 3, 21-34, 1992.

Lago, C. and Thompson, J. 1996 **Race, Culture and Counselling.** Buckingham: Open University Press.

Lee, C. 1994. Introductory lecture to a conference on race, culture and counselling. (unpublished) University of Sheffield, reproduced in **RACE Journal July, 1994**.

Lee, C. and Richardson, B. L. 1991. Multicultural Issues in Counselling: New Approaches to Diversity. Alexandria, VA: American Association for Counselling and Development.

Lee, M.Y. et al 1981. **Needs of Foreign Students from Developing Nations at U.S. Colleges and Universities**. Washington DC: NAFSA.

Leong, F. and Chou, E. Counselling International Students in Pedersen, P., Draguns, J., Lonner, W. Trimble, J. (ed.) 1996, **Counselling Across Cultures** 4th edition., London: Sage Publications.

Leong, F. 1984. **Counselling International Students** Ann Arbor: ERIC Counselling and Personnel Services Clearinghouse.

Lewins, H. Living needs, in Kinnell (ed.) 1990 **The Learning Experiences of Overseas Students.** Buckingham: Society for Research into Higher Education and Open University Press.

Locke, D. 1992 **Increasing Multicultural Understanding.** London: Sage Publications.

Locke, D. et al Hospitality begins with the invitation: Counselling Foreign Students.
Journal of Multicultural Counselling and Development, 15, 115-119.

Lomak, D. 1984 Low uptake and Non-Uptake of Counselling.: Underutilisation of Counselling Resources by Foreign Students. Unpublished dissertation. University of Texas at San Antonio.

Lowenstein, L. F. 1985 Cross-cultural Research in Relation to Counselling in Great Britain. In P. Pedersen. **Handbook of Cross-cultural Counselling and Therapy.** USA: Praeger Publishers.

Lulat, Y & Philip, G et al 1991: Government and Institutional Policy on Foreign Students: Analysis, Evaluation and Bibliography. **Special Studies In Comparative Education,** No.16, Faculty of Education Studies, State University of New York.

Lysgaard, S. Adjustment In a Foreign Society :Norwegian Fulbright Grantees Visiting the United State. Institute of Social Science Research Oslo, Norway. **International Social Science Bulletin,** 7, 45-51, 1955.

Makinde, O. 1984. **Fundamentals of Guidance and Counselling.** UK: Macmillan Publishers.

Macrae, M. The Induction of International Students to Academic Life in the United Kingdom in McNamara, D. and Harris, R (Ed) 1997 **Overseas Students in Higher Education.** London: Routledge,

McNamara, D. and Harris, R (Ed) 1997 **Overseas Students in Higher Education.** London: Routledge.

Mckinlay, N. and Stevenson, J. A Re-evaluation of Cultural Orientation **Journal of International Education.** 5(3) 7-19, 1994.
Magder, B . Multicultural Counselling **TESL TALK** pg. 58-64, 1983.

Marshall, D. Implications for Intercultural Counselling. **Multiculturalism.** 3, 9-13, 1979.

Makepeace, E. 1989 Overseas Students: Challenges of Institutional Adjustment. Standing Conference on Educational Development Paper 56, Birmingham: SCED Publications.

Manese, J. et al.1988 Needs and Perceptions of Female and Male International Undergraduate Students. **Journal of Multicultural Counselling and Development,** p25-29, 1988.

Manese, J. Leong, F and Sedlacek, 1985. Background attitudes and needs of undergraduate international students. **College Student Affairs Journal**, 6(1), 19-28.

Marketing Strategies. From **Higher Education Digest,** Summer 1993, issue 16 Quality Support Centre, Open University. Milton Keynes.

Mohamed, O. Counselling for Excellence: Adjustment Development of South-East Asia Students. in McNamara, D. and Harris, R (Ed) 1997 **Overseas Students in Higher Education** London: Routledge.

Morris, R & Christopoulos M (edited) 1988 **Helping Overseas Students To Succeed** Nottingham: NACOSA.

Morgan, D. 1988 **Focus Groups as Qualitative Research.** London: Sage Publications.

National Postgraduate Committee 1995 Guidelines for Codes of Practice for Postgraduate Research (2nd Edition), Brandon House, Troon, Ayrshire.

Nadya, A. F. Training Counsellors to Counsel International Students: Are We Ready? **The Counselling Psychologist**, .19 (1) 66-71, 1991.

Nasri, W. The Visible College The International Students: What Do We Owe Them? An Educators Reflection. **Journal of Education For Library Information Science.** 34 (1) 75-78, 1993.

Ngaio, G. Issues on Overseas Students **Higher Education** 17 , 26//11/92

Niven, A. 1988 Responsible Recruitment in Smith, P. (ed.) 1988 **The Fairground of the Market.** London: UKCOSA Publication.

Nwachukwu, U.T. & Ivey A.E Culture-Specific Counselling: An Alternative Training Model. **Journal of Counselling and Development,** 70, 106-111, 1991.

Nwachukwu, Uchenna. 1989. Culture-specific Counselling: The Igbo Case. Unpublished dissertation, University of Massachusetts at Amherst.

Oberg, K. Culture Shock: Adjustment To New Cultural Environment. **Practical Anthropology** 7, 177-182, 1960.

Okorocha E. 1982 Teaching and Learning in Higher Education: A Survey of Students and Staff views of Teaching and Learning at The Department of Religious Studies and Divinity Faculty, University of Aberdeen, Scotland. Unpublished Project Report.

Okorocha, E. 1990 A Survey of the Predominant Problems of Students at Ahmadu Bello University, Nigeria. Unpublished Master's Degree Thesis.

Okorocha, E. 1994 Barriers To Effective Counselling of Overseas Students: Implications for Cross-cultural counselling Paper Presented at the Society For Research Into Higher Education (SRHE) annual conference, University of York Dec.19, 1994.

Okorocha, E. 1995 Factors that Limit the Effectiveness of Pastoral Care and Counselling of People of Other Faiths and Cultures. Paper Presented at the Cambridge Theological Federation. Cambridge Jan 16, 1995.

Okorocha, E. Some Cultural and Communication Issues in Working with International Students. **Journal of International Education.** August 1996 7(2) 31-38, 1996.

Okorocha, E. The International Student Experience: Expectations and Realities. **Journal of Graduate Education.** 2 (3) 80-84, 1996.

Okorocha, E. Cultural Clues to Student Guidance. **Times Higher Education Supplement** (THES) 7/6/96 p13. 1996.

Okorocha, E. Coping with Cultural Differences **Study UK Postgraduate.** Hobsons Publishers, Cambridge. p8-9, Issue 4, Spring 1996.

Okorocha, E. Some Factors That Limit the Effective Counselling of Overseas Students: Implications for Cross-Cultural Counselling Paper presented at a European Conference on **Culture and Psyche in Transition.** Published by ASC in association with Forum Europeen de l'Orientation Academique (FEDORA) 82-85, March 1996.

Okorocha, E.1997 **Supervising International Research Students.** Issues in Postgraduate Supervision, Teaching and Management. No.1. London: SRHE and THES Publication. **2nd Edition 2007.**

Okorocha, E. Counselling International Students. **Journal of Race and Cultural Education in Counselling** (RACE) 12, 26-27, 1997.

Oppenheim, A.N. 1992 **Questionnaire Design, Interviewing and Attitude Measurement.** London: New Edition Pinter Publishers.

Overseas Student Trust (OST) 1978 Freedom to Study: Requirement of Overseas Students in the UK. Report of a survey for OST 1976-77 by Read, B. Hulton,J and Bazalgette, J. The Grubb Institute: An OST publication.

OST 1987. The next Steps: Overseas Students Policy into the 1990. London: OST.

Paar, Bradley & Bingi Concerns and Feelings of International Students. **Journal of College Student**, 33, 20-25, 1992.

Patton, M.Q 1991. **Qualitative Evaluation and Research Method.** 2nd edition, Newbury Park, California: Sage Publication.

Parlette, M. New Evaluation. **Trends In Education**. 34,13-18, 1974.

Pedersen, P. Counselling International Students. **The Counselling Psychologist,**
19 (1), 10-58, 1991.

Pedersen, P., Draguns, J., Lonner, W. Trimble, J. (ed.) 1996. **Counselling Across Cultures** 4th edition. London: Sage Publications.

Pedersen, P. Culture-Centred Ethical Guidelines for Counsellors' in Ponterotto, J., Casas, J., Suzuki, L. & Alexander, C (eds.) 1995. **Handbook of Multicultural Counselling.** London: Sage Publications.

Pedersen, P. (ed.) 1987. **Handbook of Cross-cultural Counselling and Therapy** USA: Praeger Publications.

Pease, A. 1995. **Body Language.** Australia: Camel Publishing Company.

Perkins et al.1977. A Comparison of the Adjustment Problems of Three International Student Groups **Journal of College Student Personnel,** 382-387. Sept.1977.

Ponterotto, J., Casas, J., Suzuki, L. & Alexander, C (eds.) 1995. **Handbook of Multicultural Counselling.** London: Sage Publications.

Pritchard, R.M.O. Amae and The Japanese Learner of English: An Action Research Study' Language, Culture and Curriculum8, (3), 249-264, 1995.

Patel, G. 1988 What We Learn from Overseas Students' in Smith, P. (ed.) **The Fairground of the Market.** London: UKCOSA Publication.

Padilla, A; Ruiz, R Alvarez, R. Community mental health services for Spanish-speaking/surnamed population. **American Psychologist** 30, 892-905, 1975.

Roberts and Higgins 1992. **Higher Education: The Student Experience.** HEIST and PCAS.

Rogers, C. & Smith, C. Identifying the need of Overseas Students: A monitoring exercise at the University of Southampton. **Journal of International Education,** 3(3)7-25, 1992.

Salmon, P 1992 **Achieving a PhD: Ten Students' Experience.** Staffordshire: Trentham Books Ltd,

Schild, E. The Foreign Student, as Stranger, learning the Norms of the Host-Culture. **Journal of Social Issues,** 21(3) 289-296, 1962

Sen, A. 1970 **Problems of Overseas Students and Nurses.** National Foundation For Educational Research In England And Wales. Sussex: King, Thorne & Stace.

Stevenson, J. Market Forces and Pre-Arrival Information for Overseas Students. **Journal of International Education** 3 (1) 35-46, 1992.

Sielski, L M Understanding Body Language. **Personnel and Guidance Journal,** v.57:238-242, 1979.

Smawfield, D. The Supervisor of Overseas Students: A Bridge Between Cultures. **Journal of Institution of Education**. Aspects of Education. 39, 51-61, 1989.

Strauss and Corbin 1990. **Basics of Qualitative Research.** London: Sage Publication.

Smith, A. 1991 Overseas Students in UK Education. (Labour Party perspective) **Journal of international Education** 2,(2), 19-27, 1991.

Strinati, D. 1995. **Popular Culture.** London: Routledge.

Sue, D. and Sue, D.W. Barriers To Effective Cross-Cultural Counselling. **Journal of Counselling Psychology,** 24 (5) 420-429, 1977.

Sue, D.W. Counselling The Culturally Different: a Conceptual Analysis. **Personnel and Guidance Journal,** 422-425, 1977.

Sue, D. W. 1990 **Counselling The Culturally Different: Theory and Practice** 2nd edition. USA: John Wiley and Sons.

Sue, S. et al 1982. The Mental Health of Asian American. San Francisco: Jossey-Brass.

Shotnes, S. (ed.) 1985 **Overseas Students Who Learns What.** London: UKCOSA Publications.

Shotnes (ed.) 1986 **Orientation :A Practical Guide For Those Working With Overseas Students.** London: UKCOSA Publication.

Shotnes (ed.) 1987 **Overseas Students - Destination UK?.** London: UKCOSA Publication.

Smith, D. Cooper, C. and Casement, A. (1996) 'Psychodynamic Therapy' in Dryden, W.(ed.) 1996. **Handbook of Individual Therapy.** London: Sage Publication.

Todd, E. Supervising Overseas Students: Problem or Opportunity? in McNamara, D. and Harris, R (Ed) (1997) **Overseas Students in Higher Education.** London: Routledge.

United Kingdom Council for Overseas Student Affairs (1992) **Orientation Within the Institution.** London: UKCOSA.

UKCOSA, 1985. **Containing Crisis: The Response to Overseas Groups in Hardship**. London: UKCOSA.

UKCOSA, 1989. Advisers' Briefing: National Group. UKCOSA News, 21, 9-15.

Van Deurzen-Smith, E. Alienation and Adaptation: First-hand experience of Student migration. Paper presented at a European Conference on **Culture and Psyche in Transition.** Published by ASC in association with Forum Europeen de l'Orientation Academique (FEDORA) 1-3, March 1996.

Van Deurzen-Smith, E. 1996. Existential Therapy in Dryden, Windy (ed.) 1996 **Handbook of Individual Therapy.** London: Sage Publications.

Vontress, C. 1971. Racial differences: Impediments to Rapport. **Journal of Counselling Psychology** 18, 7-13. 1971.

Wan, T. et al Academic Stress of International Students Attending U.S. Universities. **Journal of Research into Higher Education.** 33 (5) 607-625, 1992.

Westwood, M.J. Cross-cultural counselling: Some Special Problems and Recommendations for the Canadian Counsellor, **Canadian Counsellor**, 117 (2) 62-66 1983.

Williams, R. 1983 **Keywords: A vocabulary of Culture and Society**. London: Fontana.

Wilson, D. Overseas Students in the UK Private Sector. **Journal of International Education** 3 (2) 9-19, 1992.

Williams, L. The Overseas Students Trust 1961-1992. **UKCOSA Journal Issue** 6, 14-17, 1992

Williams, P. (ed.) 1981 The Overseas Students Question: Studies for a Policy. OST, London: Heinemann Educational Books Ltd.

Williams, R. 1983 **Keywords: A Vocabulary of Culture and Society**. London: Fontana.

Wolcott, H. 1990 **Writing Up Qualitative Research**. London: Sage Publications.

Wolfgang, A and Waxer, P. Training Counsellors to Enhance Their Sensitivity to Nonverbal Behaviour in Samuda, R. and Wolfgang A. (ed.) Intercultural Counselling and Assessment. Philosophical and Theoretical Concept, **Global Perspectives.** 6, 325-393, 1985.

Wrenn, C. 1966. The Culturally Encapsulated Counsellor. **Harvard Educational Review,** 32, 444-449.

Yamamoto, J. James, Q.; Palley N. Cultural Problems in Psychiatric Therapy. **Archives of General Psychiatry**, 19, 45-49, 1968.

Yates, A. (ed.) 1971. Students from Overseas. UK: National Foundation for Education Research in England and Wales.

Zwingmann, C and Gunn, A. 1983. **Uprooting and Health: Psychosocial Problems of Students From Abroad**. Geneva: World Health Organisation.

www.ingramcontent.com/pod-product-compliance
Lightning Source LLC
Chambersburg PA
CBHW070909160426
43193CB00011B/1410